From My Heart to the Throne For Boys

(Children's Scripture Confessions & Prayers)

Lizzy Marie Helfrich

Dedication

To my amazing husband, Brian, who has stood faithfully and patiently by my side throughout the duration of this book and whose prayers and love have not only changed my life, but has brought this life-long vision to pass.

To all my amazing children here on this earth, family, and friends that have given me the inspiration and heart to share my experiences and dedicate my life for.

To my two children, Jessica and Zechariah, who already dwell in the gates of Heaven, I know you are always by my side as I feel your presence with me each day. You are my hope and joy.

To my loving savior and Lord, Jesus Christ, who has never left me nor forsaken me. My heart will always belong to you. Your faithfulness takes my breath away. I love you.

Preface

Too often I hear stories from children telling me about their every day struggles, or even more alarming; their paranormal experiences. I also hear them talk about how often they're ill or being bullied. I can hear the defeat and sadness in their voices and I can see it in their eyes. I know exactly what they're going through because of my own past experiences at their age. I would have given anything to have had the knowledge of the power of the name of Jesus and his word as a child; which is why I was stirred to write this book. I want to assist today's children, pre-teens, and youth on how to defeat the enemy and his lies. It's important that they gain the keys to overcome and be victorious against everything that comes against them.

The enemy has reaped havoc in our homes and schools. And yes, even our Christ-centered schools. It's important that our children know there's an enemy; but even more importantly, that they gain a greater understanding of the power of the name of Jesus. The role of the Spirit of God must also be understood in order to live victoriously. As it stands, the youth of today are delving into occultism like never before. These dangers must be addressed. In reality, our youth are actually craving the supernatural power of God but are instead finding more opportunities available to them to engage in the sinister side of the supernatural. We must educate them about the truths and dangers, as well as provide them with the tools needed to overcome. This can only be done by the word of God.

Bottom line, there *is* a devil and he's out to steal, kill, and to destroy what God has put within our children's destiny's. It's my heartfelt prayer that this book of confessions and testimonials opens the spiritual eyes of your child – as well as yours. I pray that your family would gain a greater hunger and understanding for the word of God and his son – Jesus Christ – the anointed one and his anointing; author and finisher of our faith.

Table of Contents

Angel Visitor

Angel Visitor 1
Testimony by Lizzy

One day when I sat beside my granddaughter's bed while saying our nighttime prayers, to the right side of me I saw a very bright flash. It lasted only a second or two, but was so bright that I remember even with my eyes closed, it lid up the entire room. My granddaughter, who had her eyes open but looking the other direction, described a very bright yet soft flash of light. She also saw it light up the entire room in a glow. She said that it did not hurt her eyes at all even though it was so bright. As we were describing what we had just seen, we could feel the entire air in the room became very still. We both felt a presence in the room with us. It was the most peaceful feeling we had ever felt. We didn't want to move because we felt like we would swoosh it away. It was a very holy moment. We knew that an angel was there with us and that God wanted us to know that he was hearing our prayers. That night we felt God's love in a way we had never felt before. We have never forgotten this event. By the way, just to make sure it wasn't lightning or anything like that (though we knew it wasn't), I walked over to the window near the front door of the bedroom and sure enough, there was not a single cloud in the sky. It was a clear and warm evening. I've heard of other stories of angels appearing as flashes of light during prayer meetings. How exciting that it had happened to us, too!

Angel Visitor 2
Testimony by Grace

One day when I was sitting on my bed before school, I saw two round white and bluish bright lights that all of a sudden came down from my ceiling and landed on the carpet. The beautiful lights stayed there for just a few seconds and then got sucked back up into the ceiling and left. I instantly felt so happy and giggly. There was this really nice peace that came on me when I saw the glowing lights. As soon as they left, I ran into my parent's room to tell them what had happened. We were so happy together because we felt I had been visited by an angel, letting me know that I'm always being watched and protected. You see, I always do my best to read my bible and pray before school. I also say scriptures every day. God's angels love God's word and wait for you to speak them so they can begin to work on your behalf. Make sure to keep them busy. ☺

Bless the Lord, ye his angels, that excel in strength, that do his commandments, hearkening unto the voice of his word.   Psalms 103:20

10

Anger

ANGRY
When I Feel Angry

We must stop being angry, mean, and evil. We should no longer say things that hurt people's feelings or make fun of them.

But now ye also put off all these; anger, wrath, malice, blasphemy, filthy communication out of your mouth.
Colossians 3:8

If someone wants to argue and fight with you, remember that God tells us to say something calm back. This will make the fight stop. If you say something mean or rude back, it will make things worse.

A soft answer turneth away wrath: but grievous words stir up anger.
Proverbs 15:1

If you're careful to watch what you say, you will save yourself from getting into a lot of trouble. Stay calm and be the mature one.

Whoso keepeth his mouth and his tongue keepeth his soul from troubles.
Proverbs 21:23

God says that intelligent people don't say too many words during conversations. When you're around people, be the one to say the least words. More words stir lies.

He that hath knowledge spareth his words: and a man of understanding is of an excellent spirit.
Proverbs 17:27

You can be angry (toward the enemy by
defeating him with the word of God),
but make sure not to sin by throwing
things, being rude, holding a grudge,
or getting revenge. Instead, pray
and don't go to bed mad.
Don't open the door
to the devil.

Be ye angry, and sin not: let not the sun
go down upon your wrath: v. 27 Neither
give place to the devil.   Ephesians 4:26-27

Prayer

Father God, I come to you in the name of Jesus and ask that you please help me not to sin when I get angry. I thank you that you have given me the patience & self-control that I need to stay peaceful. Thank you that I can come to you for help to overcome at any time.

Please forgive me for getting so angry and then purposely staying mad. Instead of directing that anger towards the enemy and defeating the situation with the word of God, I gossiped about it and said things I shouldn't have. There have even been times that I've talked back to my parents, family, and friends. I've really been in a bad mood about everything and I know this is not okay with you. Please help me not to be angry anymore. I can't do it without your help. I repent for not obeying your word and thank you that I'm forgiven now because your word says that if we come to you and ask for forgiveness, you will forgive us. Thank you for your love for us.

In Jesus Name...Amen

When was a time that you got really mad and did something you shouldn't have? What better choice could you have made that would have pleased the Lord?

_____

_____

_____

_____

_____

_____

_____

_____

_____

Bad Thoughts

BAD THOUGHTS
When I Get Bad Thoughts

Fill your minds only with good thoughts. Thoughts that are true, loving, always honest and not sinful. If Jesus would be happy with your thoughts, then think about those things and not bad ones.

<u>Finally, brethren, whatsoever things are true, whatsoever things are honest, whatsoever things are just, whatsoever things are pure, whatsoever things are lovely, whatsoever things are of good report; if there be any virtue, and if there be any praise, think on these things.</u>   Philippians 4:8

When bad or evil thoughts start coming into your mind, they are most likely from the devil so make sure to cast them out in Jesus name. Immediately think about something good like God's word. Don't let your mind wander on evil. You can control those thoughts with Jesus help. Besides, we don't really fight against people; we are actually at war with evil spirits. Thankfully, Jesus already beat the devil at the cross.

<u>For though we walk in the flesh, we do not war after the flesh: v. 4 (For the weapons of our warfare are not carnal, but mighty through God to the pulling down of strong holds;) v. 5 Casting down imaginations, and every high thing that exalteth itself against the knowledge of God, and bringing into captivity every thought to the obedience of Christ.</u>   2 Corinthians 10:3-5

God gave us the same Holy Spirit that Jesus has so we could be guided and instructed by his ways. Jesus knew that only through his Spirit could we live this life on earth victoriously, having his ways of Godly thinking.

For who hath known the mind of the Lord, that he may instruct him? But we have the mind of Christ.

1 Corinthians 2:16

_____

_____

_____

_____

_____

_____

_____

_____

_____

_____

_____

_____

_____

_____

_____

_____

_____

_____

_____

_____

_____

_____

Prayer

Father God, I come to you in the name of Jesus and ask that you please give me strength to overcome when I get bad thoughts. I know that evil thoughts only hurt people and even us, so I ask that you would please keep me strong during these times. Help me when I think about hurting people's feelings or getting a plan in my head to do something that is mean.

Please help me to always do my best to walk in the fruits of the Spirit, especially in self-control. Thank you for answering my prayers and for teaching me to do what is right through your word. Lastly, I declare that I have the mind of Christ and cast down every useless imagination that tries to rise up against the word.

In Jesus Name...Amen

Rebuke bad thoughts quickly
before they turn into sin &
birth in your heart. Use
God's word to replace
the bad thoughts;
otherwise, you'll
give into
them.

Replace the above words with good words about who God says you are to him:

_____   _____

_____   _____

_____   _____

_____   _____

_____   _____

_____   _____

Bad Words

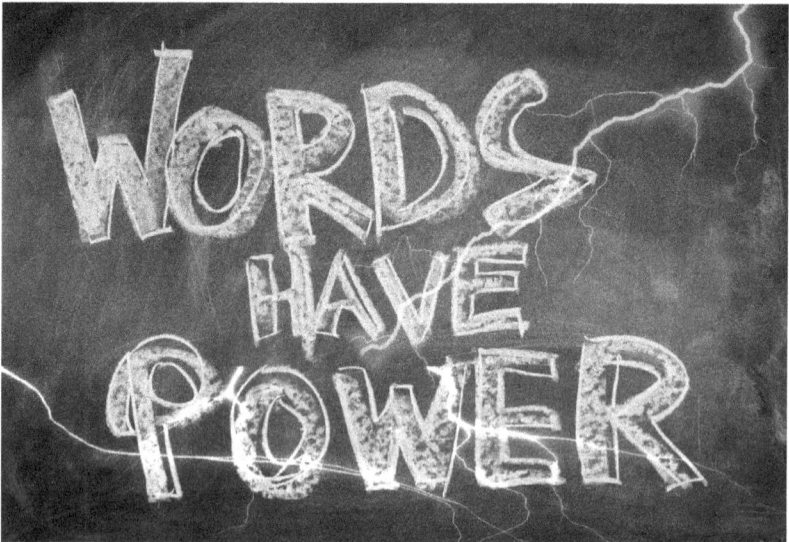

BAD WORDS
Is Cursing Really That Bad?

Do not ever use filthy curse words because God says very clearly that they are dumb and immature. Instead of being a follower by speaking the bad words others might say, be a leader and speak words of thankfulness and all that the Lord has done for you.

Neither filthiness, nor foolish talking, nor jesting, which are not convenient: but rather giving of thanks.

Ephesians 5:4

Stop using curse words and saying things that are not good and hurt others. Only say nice things that will make someone feel better and help them be encouraged. You help others this way. Our tongues hold life and death in them. Speak kind words so that life will flow out of you.

Let no corrupt communication proceed out of your mouth, but that which is good to the use of edifying, that it may minister grace unto the hearers.

Ephesians 4:29

With our tongues we praise God and curse people. They are his creation and made after him. How can we bless and curse people with the same mouth.

Therewith bless we God, even the Father; and therewith curse we men, which are made after the similitude of God. V. 10 Out of the same mouth proceedeth blessing and cursing. My brethren, these things ought not so to be.

James 3:9-10

Be very careful what words you say because God says that whatever comes out of your mouth is really coming out of your heart. These words could ruin your whole self; spirit, body, and soul.

But those things which proceed out of the mouth come forth from the heart; and they defile the man.
Matthew 15:18

If you think you'll be safe cursing about someone in a quiet area like your house, be careful because you never know whose listening and will go off and tell on you. It is better to not talk about anyone.

Curse not the king, no not in thy thought and curse not the rich in thy bedchamber: for a bird of the air shall carry the voice, and that which hath wings shall tell the matter.
Ecclesiastes 10:20

God does not want us to be swearing or making promises by things in heaven or on earth. So don't tell someone, "I swear by the heavens above that what I'm telling you is the truth." When you say something, just let your yes be a yes and your no a no. Besides, heaven belongs to God.

But I say unto you, Swear not at all; neither by heaven; for it is God's throne.
Matthew 5:34

We should not make promises by things in heaven or earth. Don't ever swear by the moon and stars, or anything else. If you say anything more than a simple yes or no, you could fall under judgment. **But above all things, my brethren, swear not, neither by heaven, neither by the earth, neither by any other oath: but let your yea be yea; and your nay, nay; lest ye fall into condemnation.**
James 5:12

Always remember that it's not what goes into your mouth that makes you unhealthy for worship to God, but it's the bad things that come out of your mouth because this means they're already in your heart.

Not that which goeth into the mouth defileth a man; but that which cometh out of the mouth, this defileth a man. Matthew 15:11

Anyone who thinks they are spiritual by keeping holy days or rituals, but cannot control their own tongue, only fools themselves and the religion they practice is empty and useless.

If any man among you seem to be religious, and bridleth not his tongue, but deceiveth his own heart, this man's religion is vain. James 1:26

_____
_____
_____
_____
_____
_____
_____
_____
_____
_____
_____
_____
_____
_____
_____
_____
_____
_____
_____

Prayer

Father God, I come to you in the name of Jesus and ask you to please help me not to say curse words. I know these words don't please you and make you disappointed in me. They also don't make me look like a Christian and I instantly become a bad example. I'm sure that neither God, Jesus, nor the Holy Spirit speaks bad words since bad words come from the devil.

Please give me the strength to speak words that please you. I'll make sure to be a good influence and speak only the words you want me to speak, and not the words that others want me to speak.

In Jesus Name...Amen

How can you sing God's praises and say
curse words with the same tongue?
Would you be okay cursing right in
front of Jesus? The Lord
calls cursing immature.
It also breaks
his heart.

Bullied

BULLIED
When I'm Being Made Fun of & Scared

Even if you feel alone, do not fear because God is always with you. God will make you strong and will help you. Anyone that is angry with you will feel ashamed and be totally embarrassed. God says he'll protect you and chase all your enemies away from you. The mean people that are bullying you or threatening you will disappear.

Fear thou not; for I am with thee: be not dismayed; for I am thy God: I will strengthen thee; yea, I will help thee; yea, I will uphold thee with the right hand of my righteousness.   Isaiah 41:10

If someone is mean to you, act like Jesus would and love them. Instead of doing bad to them like they did to you, do something good. If they lie and say evil things, pray for them. This is what Jesus would want us to do.

But I say unto you which hear, Love your enemies, do good to them which hate you, v. 28 Bless them that curse you, and pray for them which despitefully use you.   Luke 6:27-28

Living at peace with people can be hard, but if you can help it, do your best to get along with them; especially, your enemies. Don't start fights or look for revenge. God would rather you feed your enemy if he's hungry, or give him something to drink if he's thirsty. This way they'll know you really have Jesus in you.

If it be possible, as much as lieth in you, live peaceably with all men. v. 19 Dearly beloved, avenge not yourselves, but rather give place unto wrath: for it is written, Vengeance is mine; I will repay, saith the Lord. v. 20 Therefore if thine enemy hunger, feed him; if he thirst, give him drink: for in so doing thou shalt heap coals of fire on his head. v. 21 Be not overcome of evil, but overcome evil with good.   Romans 12:18-21

People are not what we really fight against. We are really at war with evil spirits; though people do allow them to work through them at times. God tells us to arm ourselves; using his weapons of truth, peace, faith, righteousness, and salvation. Pray for one another, too. For we wrestle not against flesh and blood, but against principalities, against powers, against the rulers of the darkness of this world, against spiritual wickedness in high places. v. 13 Wherefore take unto you the whole armour of God, that ye may be able to withstand in the evil day, and having done all to stand. v. 14 Stand therefore, having your loins girt about with truth, and having on the breastplate of righteousness; v. 15 And your feet shod with the preparation of the gospel of peace; v. 16 Above all, taking the shield of faith, wherewith ye shall be able to quench all the fiery darts of the wicked. v. 17 And take the helmet of salvation, and the sword of the Spirit, which is the word of God: v. 18 Praying always with all prayer and supplication in the Spirit, and watching thereunto with all perseverance and supplication for all saints.   Ephesians 6:12-18

Jesus had never done anything bad to anyone; yet, while the people were hurting and crucifying him on the cross, Jesus still asked God to forgive them anyway. We must follow his example of forgiveness.

Then said Jesus, Father, forgive them; for they know not what they do. And they parted his raiment, and cast lots. Luke 23:34

Though you may be going through a lot of bad things in your life, like being bullied, God's power will always be there with you to make sure you're safe from your enemies. Remember that you're never alone. He's there.

Though I walk in the midst of trouble, thou wilt revive me: thou shalt stretch forth thine hand against the wrath of mine enemies, and thy right hand shall save me. Psalms 138:7

_____

_____

_____

_____

_____

_____

_____

_____

_____

_____

_____

_____

_____

Prayer

Father God, I come to you in the name of Jesus and thank you that your word says that I'm always protected by you. I know that you also send your angels to protect me. Help me to trust that you will keep me safe when anyone is being mean to me or I'm being bullied.

Please give me the strength to tell an adult if I'm ever being bullied or am in a dangerous situation. Even if someone is cyber bullying me on the computer. I know that you care for me very much so right now I declare that I will trust in the Lord and in the power of his strength to save and protect me from my enemies or anyone that tries to hurt me.

In Jesus Name...Amen

Being bullied makes a person feel as
if they're worth nothing. Jesus
died for us because he loves
us & wanted us to know how
important we are; especially,
to him. Let's show that
love back to
others.

Ephesians Prayers

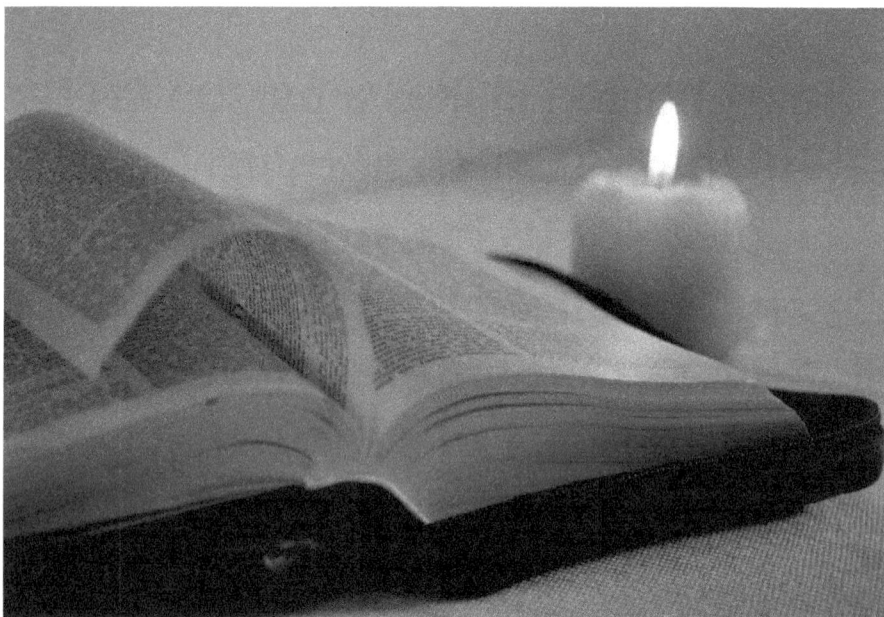

Ephesians Prayers
(Paul's Prayer for Spiritual Wisdom)

- Paul's prayer was sent up to God our Father in the name of Jesus.
- Paul prayed all the time for the church at Ephesus. He loved them.
- Paul had others pray along with him. They were followers of Christ like he was.
- Paul thanked God for these people because he knew God loved them.
- Paul prayed that they would know God much more than he ever did.
- Paul prayed that they would understand the hope of what they do.
- Paul prayed that they would have wisdom & understand of his word.
- Paul prayed that they would understand that the word was everything.
- Paul prayed that the eyes of their heart would see clearly.
- Paul prayed that they would understand the Holy Spirit's power within them.
- Paul prayed that the mysteries of God would be shown to them.
- Paul prayed that they would understand their eternal glory and future.
- Paul prayed all this for the people at that time and for all of us alive up to this very day.

Ephesians 1:15-23

When I heard of your wonderful faith in the Lord Jesus and your amazing love for those who follow him, I was so very happy that I couldn't stop thanking God for you! Every single time I pray I think of all of you and just have to shout huge thanks. But I want you all to know something, I don't only *thank* God for all of you, but I ask the precious God of our Master, Jesus Christ, the beautiful God of glory to give you wisdom; having clear understanding of personal fellowship with him. I ask that all of your eyes would be super sharp and clear to see like that of an eagle's so you can know exactly what he's called you to do on the earth, having a firm grip on the hugeness of his magnificent way of life that he has for all of us that follow him daily. To those of us who believe in him, he works great power within us. All of our strength comes from Christ because God raised him from the dead and set him way up high in heaven, sitting him right next to him at his right hand and putting him (Jesus) in charge of running the whole universe and everyone in it. There's no other name or king that is greater than his. No demons, rulers, or even the devil's power is higher than the authority found in Jesus. And every single thing that has a name is also under the name of Jesus. It will be this way forever and ever! God put everything under Jesus' feet and made him the head over all things to the church which is his body, the biggest part of him that fills everything completely.

Wherefore I also, after I heard of your faith in the Lord Jesus, and love unto all the saints, V. 16 Cease not to give thanks for you, making mention of you in my prayers; V. 17 That the God of our Lord Jesus Christ, the Father of glory, may give unto you the spirit of wisdom and revelation in the knowledge of him: V. 18 The eyes of your understanding being enlightened; that ye may know what is the hope of his calling, and what the riches of the glory of inheritance in the saints, V. 19 And what is the exceeding greatness of his power to usward who believe, according to the working of his mighty power, V.20 Which he wrought in Christ, when he raised him from the dead, and set him at his own right hand in the heavenly places, V. 21 Far above all principality, and power, and might, and dominion, and every name that is named, not only in this world, but also in that which is to come: V. 22 And hath put all things under his feet, and gave him to be the head over all things to the church, V. 23 Which is his body, the fullness of him that filleth all in all.

Prayer

Father God, I come to you in the name of Jesus and thank you that I can come to you anytime I need answers about my everyday life, as well as for my calling. I know that you have very special things that you want me to do here on earth so I ask that you would please give me the wisdom to be successful. Please open my eyes so that I will be able to see exactly what it is you want me to do in this life and with my future.

One more thing, since I know that your wisdom is huge, I ask that you please help me to do well in school. Especially, when I take a test or am having a hard time understanding certain subjects like math or grammar. Thank you for answering my prayers according to your word.

In Jesus Name...Amen

Example

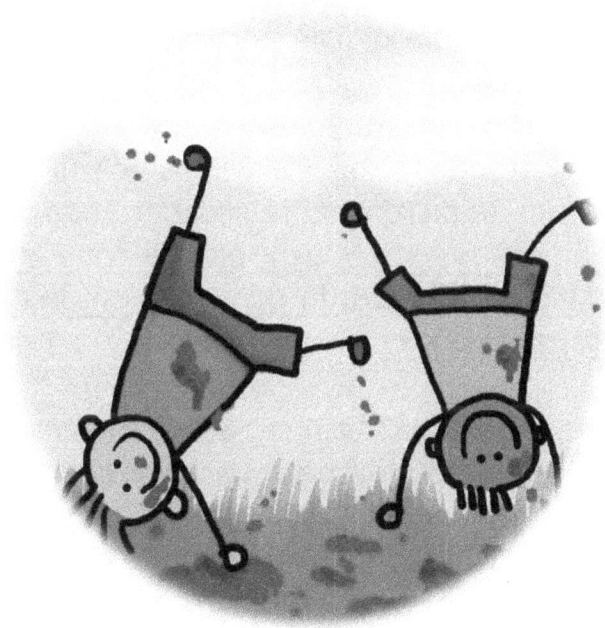

EXAMPLE
Being a Good Example

Act well and be kind before everyone so when they see that you are peaceful and kind, they will give God all the glory and know that he really is real.

Let your light so shine before men, that they may see your good works, and glorify your Father which is in heaven. Matthew 5:16

Even though you are still young, don't let anyone treat you like you're not important. Even as young as you are, you can be a good example and role model for other believers on how they should be living – even your parents. Do this by saying good things, walking in love, being strong in your faith, and living a holy life that does not like to sin. Be different. Be a leader...not a follower.

Let no man despise thy youth; but be thou an example of the believers, in word, in conversation, in charity, in spirit, in faith, in purity. 1 Timothy 4:12

A lot of kids and adults want to act like everyone else so they can fit in. They'll even say bad words or smoke just so they can be liked, but God tells us to not become like the people of the world that love to sin and do bad things. Instead, he wants you to change your way of thinking to his way. Study God's word so you will know what is good and acceptable to him and even his perfect will for you.

I beseech you therefore, brethren, by the mercies of God, that ye present your bodies a living sacrifice, holy, acceptable unto God, which is your reasonable service. v. 2 And be not conformed to this world: but be ye transformed by the renewing of your mind, that ye may prove what is that good, and acceptable, and perfect, will of God.   Romans 12:1-2

_____

_____

_____

_____

_____

_____

_____

_____

_____

_____

_____

_____

_____

_____

_____

_____

_____

_____

_____

_____

_____

_____

_____

Prayer

Father God, I come to you in the name of Jesus and thank you that your word tells us to always be a good example for others so they can see that Jesus lives in us. Lord, I thank you that by the power of the Holy Spirit we can be the best examples we can possibly be. We know that being kind, not lying, walking in love, and not constantly arguing with others is a very good way of being a good example.

Lord, please help us to stay at peace during rough times. Help us to always be happy and thankful for all you've given us. We know that in doing these things, we can shine like Jesus. We thank you for your strength in us knowing that we can do all these things through Christ who strengthens us.

In Jesus Name...Amen

Faith

FAITH
When I Need Help Believing

God tells us that faith believes something already happened without even having to see it first. So when we pray and ask God for something like needing healing in our bodies, if we will just believe that our prayers have already been answered, then they will be.

Now faith is the substance of things hoped for, the evidence of things not seen.   Hebrews 11:1

The Lord says that if you have faith as small as a mustard seed, which is almost as small as a grain of sand, then you can do great things for God.

And the Lord said, If ye had faith as a grain of mustard seed, ye might say unto this sycamine tree, Be thou plucked up by the root, and be thou planted in the sea; and it should obey you.   Luke 17:6

The whole world we live in was first made by faith, then spoken. Everything we see like plants, oceans, trees, and animals were made by faith first then became reality. People and even teachers will tell you that the world just kind of happened by some huge "Big Bang" in space, but that's not true. God created the earth and heavens all by faith. We don't believe in evolution but only in creation because God created it all. Through faith we understand that the worlds were framed by the word of God, so that things which are seen were not made of things which do appear.   Hebrews 11:3

A very sick woman with blood problems knew that if she could just touch even the bottom of Jesus' clothes, she would be healed. When she did, Jesus felt power come out of him & she was healed instantly.

<u>And Jesus said, Somebody hath touched me: for I perceive that virtue is gone out of me.</u>   Luke 8:46

If two or three of you get together to pray and believe for something, God will answer your prayers if you pray according to his will & in faith. Also, if two or more of you are together and talking, praying, or worshiping Jesus, he is right there between all of you.

<u>Again I say unto you, That if two of you shall agree on earth as touching any thing that they shall ask, it shall be done for them of my Father which is in heaven. V. 20 For where two or three are gathered together in my name, there am I in the midst of them.</u>

          Matthew 18:19-20

If you tell a huge situation in your life to go away and believe in faith that's it gone, without doubting, you will have exactly what you asked for. Walk in faith.

<u>For verily I say unto you, That whosoever shall say unto this mountain, Be thou removed, and be thou cast into the sea; and shall not doubt in his heart, but shall believe that those things which he saith shall come to pass; he shall have whatsoever he saith.</u>   Mark 11:23

Again, the Lord tells us that whatever we desire, like writing a book or someone in your family getting saved, just believe you've received those answers when you pray and you will for sure have them.

Therefore I say unto you, What things soever ye desire, when ye pray, believe that ye receive them, and ye shall have them.   Mark 11:24

When you pray, check your heart to make sure you're not holding unforgiveness towards anyone. Make sure to forgive them if they've hurt you because the bible says that if you don't forgive them, he will not forgive you or your sins and your prayers will not be heard.

And when ye stand praying, forgive, if ye have ought against any: that your Father also which is in heaven may forgive you your trespasses. v. 26 But if ye do not forgive, neither will your Father which is in heaven forgive your trespasses.   Mark 11:25-26

The Lord always watches over his word to make sure that it comes to pass. If he says he'll do something, you can be sure that he will. He never lies.

Then said the Lord unto me, Thou hast well seen: for I will hasten my word to perform it.   Jeremiah 1:12

Hold tight to your belief as a Christian. Don't doubt God's word. We can always trust him to do what he promised. Let us hold fast the profession of our faith without wavering: (for he is faithful that promised;)
                                        Hebrews 10:23

God tells us that our faith grows stronger and stronger every time we listen to scriptures over and over again.

So then faith cometh by hearing, and hearing by the word of God.   Romans 10:17

There is absolutely nothing impossible with God.
For with God nothing shall be impossible. Luke 1:37

As Christians who believe in Jesus, we should always be walking by faith and never by what we see or don't see, physically.
(For we walk by faith, not by sight:) 2 Corinthians 5:7

If you need wisdom for school or things in your life, ask God who loves to give a lot. Remember, you have to ask him in faith without doubting. God says that if you doubt, you're like a wave that just kind of floats around getting thrown all over the ocean. If you doubt, you won't receive from God. He doesn't want you thinking two different ways. He wants you to think by faith only.
If any of you lack wisdom, let him ask of God, that giveth to all men liberally, and upbraideth not; and it shall be given him. v. 6 But let him ask in faith, nothing wavering. For he that wavereth is like a wave of the sea driven with the wind and tossed. v. 7 For let not that man think that he shall receive any thing of the Lord. v. 8 A double minded man is unstable in all his ways.
James 1:5-8

_____

_____

_____

_____

_____

_____

_____

_____

Write your own song about faith. Try and make it rhyme if you can. When you're done, sing it to God, your friends, or family and then have them sing it with you.

_____

_____

_____

_____

_____

_____

_____

_____

_____

Faith...is already seeing what you
have declared with your
spiritual eyes, before
you actually see
it with your
physical
eyes.

-Lizzy

Prayer

Father God, I come to you in the name of Jesus and thank you that you've given all of us a good measure of faith that we can cause to grow stronger and stronger. You said that if we had faith even as small as a <u>mustard</u> <u>seed</u>, we could move mountains. I have huge mountains of problems sometimes and I know that if I will just believe and have total faith in your word, then those problems in my life will have to go because you are faithful.

Father God, King David in the old testament of the bible said that he had to stir himself up at different times of his life because he had no one around him to help encourage him. When he did this, he got his faith stronger by trusting in you and always speaking your words out loud. I will do the same. Thank you that according to my faith, it will be done for me. Please give me the strength to always trust in you like all the heroes of faith in the bible.

In Jesus Name...Amen

Though a mustard seed
may be tiny, it grows
up to be a tall tree.
All the birds of the
air eat from it.
Our faith can
grow just
as big.

Favor

FAVOR
God's Open Door of Blessings

God's favor brought Joseph supernatural increase and promotion. Even in jail, he was very favored by all.
But the Lord was with Joseph, and shewed him mercy, and gave him favour in the sight of the keeper of the prison.   Genesis 39:21

God has blessed us with great favor; not only in his eyes, but in people's eyes as well. Everywhere you go, you are full of God's power, peace, and favor.
Grace be to you, and peace, from God our Father, and from the Lord Jesus Christ.   Ephesians 1:2

God will bless you in every way in order to provide for you so that you can always have plenty to give to people in need. This will cause others to thank God and believe in him because he helped them meet their needs.
Being enriched in everything to all bountifulness, which causeth through us thanksgiving to God.
                                                2 Corinthians 9:11

When you are in need of something, know that you can come before God's throne that is full of mercy and pray to him bravely. Since you have favor with him, he will help you in your time of need. **Let us therefore come boldly unto the throne of grace, that we may obtain mercy, and find grace to help in time of need.**   Hebrews 4:16

God is always able and willing to give you great favor. He blesses you with every need so you'll have more than enough to do all kinds of good deeds for others.

And God is able to make all grace abound toward you; that ye, always having all sufficiency in all things, may abound to every good work. 2 Corinthians 9:8

God will not only give you favor with your enemies, but he will restore everything those enemies took from you. That could be things like money, health, friendships, homes, or even happiness. Example: When the children of Israel were no longer slaves of Egypt, God restored everything to them and brought them out of Egypt very rich & healthy.

And I will give this people favour in the sight of the Egyptians: and it shall come to pass, that, when ye go, ye shall not go empty. Exodus 3:21

The Favor of God will give you special treatment above other people, just like he did with Esther. He'll make sure that you are treated more special than anyone else because you are his kid. Kind of like movie stars do when they go to restaurants or other places.

And the king loved Esther above all the women, and she obtained grace and favour in his sight more than all the virgins; so that he set the royal crown upon her head, and made her queen instead of Vashti. Esther 2:17

The Egyptians had hardened their hearts against God and his people so much, that they waged war against Israel as God knew they would. It was their own evil hearts that got them destroyed, as they had none of God's favor on their side.

For it was of the Lord to harden their hearts, that they should come against Israel in battle, that he might destroy them utterly, and that they might have no favour, but that he might destroy them, as the Lord commanded Moses.   Joshua 11:20

God will recognize you in front of others when you least expect it. When David was just a kid, God chose him to be the next King of Israel. He was the smallest of all his big brothers. He took care of sheep & played the harp making songs, so everyone was shocked that God had chosen him. Even King Saul found favor in David.

And Saul sent to Jesse, saying, Let David, I pray thee, stand before me; for he hath found favour in my sight.   1 Samuel 16:22

_____
_____
_____
_____
_____
_____
_____
_____
_____
_____
_____
_____
_____
_____
_____
_____
_____
_____

Testimony of God's Favor (1)

My two grandchildren and I travel a lot and used to travel way more than we do now. We would travel as "standby" passengers, which makes flying even more difficult; especially, during holidays. My two grandchildren and I would have to wait until everyone got boarded onto the airplane first and then we would get called on *only* if there were three seats left. If we didn't get on, we would be stranded in the airport for hours and hours or sometimes until the next day. On really bad trips, we would have to wait days before getting home, jumping from one airport to the other. As a manager at my job, I would often not be there on Mondays & the girls would miss school a lot.

I began studying more about the favor of God on our lives and decided to start thanking God for this favor every time we flew. I also began to quote scriptures about the favor of God out loud. After that, we always got on a flight and were never stranded at airports again! Hallelujah!

Testimony of God's Favor (2)

One year, one of my granddaughters was going on a field trip. I really wanted to go on this field trip but the only way you could be a chaperone for it was to win by a lottery contest. You had to fill out a slip with your information, and then amongst 20 or so other parents, wait to see if you had been chosen. Only one person was going to be able to chaperone along with the teachers. I began to confess that I had the favor of God on my life and that I would be "the one" chosen to go on that field trip. I knew that God gives us the desires of our hearts (as long as they're according to his will), so I stood in faith.

About 2 weeks later, one of the teachers handed me a letter and said that out of all the parents, I was the one chosen to go. Yay, God! He is so faithful! It was one of the funnest times I had ever had.

Prayer

Father God, I come to you in the name of Jesus and thank you that I am extremely blessed and highly favored by you. I thank you that everywhere I go I'm favored. I declare that I am always right where I'm supposed to be and at the exact time I'm supposed to be there. I know that you always empower me to succeed in everything I put my hands to do.

Just like Queen Esther and King David, I know that I will be treated special because I am your child. Thank you that you give me great victory over hard times in my life and that your favor for me will even cause laws and rules to change. I love you and praise you with all my heart.

In Jesus Name...Amen

Fear

FEAR
When I Am Feeling Scared

No matter what, I know the Lord is with me so I do not have to be afraid of anything or anyone. He will help me defeat my enemies.

<u>The Lord is on my side; I will not fear: what can man do unto me?</u>   Psalms 118:6

God never tries to scare us. He would never do that. He gives us good things like power to defeat the devil, love that destroys what is bad and evil, and a peaceful mind.

<u>For God hath not given us a spirit of fear; but of power, and of love, and of a sound mind.</u>   2 Timothy 1:7

You will never find fear where God is because his perfect love for you takes away all the fear if you trust in him. Fear brings suffering and torture to your mind. God only wants you to be at peace.

<u>There is no fear in love; but perfect love casteth out fear: because fear hath torment. He that feareth is not made perfect in love.</u>   1 John 4:18

God has great power so be strong in that power knowing that he will protect you with all his might.

<u>Finally, my brethren, be strong in the Lord, and in the power of his might.</u>   Ephesians 6:10

Don't ever be afraid because God is always with you. Also, don't lose hope or give up. God will help you and keep you strong.

Fear thou not; for I am with thee: be not dismayed; for I am thy God: I will strengthen thee; yea, I will help thee; yea, I will uphold thee with the right hand of my righteousness.   Isaiah 41:10

God has commanded that we be strong and not afraid. This is something he expects us to do because he knows it's good for us. So remember to trust him by not being afraid or losing hope since he goes with you everywhere you go and will strengthen you too.

Have not I commanded thee? Be strong and of a good courage; be not afraid, neither be thou dismayed: for the Lord thy God is with thee whithersoever thou goest.   Joshua 1:9

There is a great reward for those that do not lose their courage, get into fear, and stay in faith.

Cast not away therefore your confidence, which hath great recompence of reward.   Hebrews 10:35

Even if you walk through the *shadow* of a deadly valley like a really hard test, remember that it's only a *shadow* and cannot hurt you. Do not fear because the Lord Jesus is your shepherd and his staff will lead, guide, and protect you through all you do.

Yea, though I walk through the valley of the shadow of death, I will fear no evil: for thou art with me; thy rod and thy staff they comfort me.   Psalms 23:4

The name of the Lord Jesus is like a very strong tower that cannot easily be destroyed. Those that love God run into that strong tower and are always kept safe. Stay close to Jesus always.

The name of the LORD is a strong tower: the righteous runneth into it, and is safe. Proverbs 18:10

When you read God's word every day, you will know for sure that he's always with you and you will not be afraid when you hear bad news or if something scary happens to you. You'll remain full of peace, being unmovable because he's on your side.

I have set the LORD always before me: because he is at my right hand, I shall not be moved. Psalms 16:8

_____

_____

_____

_____

_____

_____

_____

_____

_____

_____

_____

_____

_____

_____

_____

_____

_____

_____

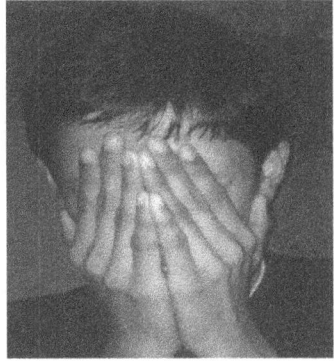

Dear Heavenly Father,

I come to you in the name of Jesus and ask you to please help me not to be scared right now because I feel very scared. I put this fear on myself for playing a game I wasn't supposed to. I also watched a scary movie knowing it would scare me. Your word says that you've not given us a spirit of fear but of power, love, and a sound mind so I speak your scriptures over me and thank you that your word is working in me. I truly do apologize for messing around with evil things. I ask you to please forgive me and help me to not be interested in these kinds of scary interests. I don't want to open the door to the enemy and allow evil things anywhere near my life. Please help me to keep my mind on peaceful things. Your word says that if we ask for forgiveness, you will forgive us. I thank you for being so kind and for keeping your word close to me. I refuse to give in to the devil like this again. I will resist him and stay away from evil.

In Jesus Name...Amen

FEAR TESTIMONY 1

When fear couldn't touch me...

My name is Gabriella. I had a really hard time always being afraid at night when I went to bed. I would have bad nightmares. They would be very, very scary. I started to pray a lot and ask God to help me. Whenever I would have a bad dream, I would scream out the name of Jesus in my dream! The more I yelled it, the more the evil looking spirits ran from me in my dreams. I started to figure out that they were really scared of me. Well, they were actually really scared of the name of Jesus, and the Jesus in me. Anyway, I wondered what would happen if I said the name of Jesus again if I did end up having another bad dream. Well, a few weeks later, I did end up getting another bad dream. I dreamt that some very ugly demon creatures were chasing me all over my house, up and down the stairs. Suddenly, I stopped running, looked at them, then began yelling out the name of Jesus and telling them to go away. Guess what? They all disappeared. I could see that some of them had gone outside and were staring through the window trying to come in but they couldn't. My prayer had chased them away.

My family always prays that God and his angels will watch over our house while we sleep and while we're away during the day. We ask God to put the blood of Jesus over our house and even our cars. I've learned that I can say the name of Jesus anytime during the day or night and he will help me. He will help you, too! If you're ever afraid or have a bad dream, speak the name of Jesus over that situation because it's the name that's above every name ever named. It's powerful! Also, remember to say scriptures every night before bed. Here are a few I say every day.

~ Confess 1 John 4:18 ~

~

~ Confess 1 Timothy 1:7 ~

FEAR TESTIMONY 2

When the spirit of fear had to flee...

Hi...My name is Eli. One time I kept getting woken up in the middle of the night by a feeling. I would try to go back to sleep but couldn't. I felt like I needed to get up so I did. I walked out of my room and then back to bed. Again, I just couldn't sleep. I felt like I needed to go back out of my room into the hallway. As soon as I did, I looked towards my sister's room and saw a tall misty creature with one red eye. It didn't notice that I was looking at it at first. I saw that it kept trying to ram itself into my sister's room, running back and forth trying to break the door down but it just couldn't. It tried to ram the door several more times when all of a sudden it noticed that I was standing there watching it. When it noticed me staring at it, straight out of my mouth I said, "Get out of here right now in Jesus name!" As soon as I said that, it disappeared. It was like smoke that kind of blows away. It disappeared into thin air just like that. I was really surprised that I didn't feel that scared. I turned right around and went back to bed. This time I was able to fall right back to sleep.

If you ask me, I'm sure that an angel was trying to wake me up and show me what was trying to enter into my sister's room. I'm glad that we always confess the blood of Jesus over our house. I'm also glad that I got up and obeyed the feeling I was having in my heart. The name of Jesus is truly the most powerful name of all!

Forgiveness

FORGIVENESS
When I Need To Forgive

God wants you to be very careful in what you do. He wants you to make sure to correct other people that believe in Jesus to stop sinning and to forgive anyone that asks you to forgive them.

Take heed to yourselves: If thy brother trespass against thee, rebuke him; and if he repent, forgive him.

Luke 17:3

If someone is rude or bullying you, ask God to bless them anyway and pray for them, even if they're being mean to you on purpose.

Bless them that curse you, and pray for them which despitefully use you.   Luke 6:28

God wants you to bless everyone that treats you bad. He wants you to bless them and walk in love with them, instead of hate.

Bless them which persecute you: bless, and curse not.

Romans 12:14

God wants you to forgive at all times. He knows that you will be able to keep your friends if you will just forgive them, but if you keep talking about what they did wrong, you will definitely lose them.

He that covereth a transgression seeketh love; but he that repeateth a matter separateth very friends.

Proverbs 17:9

During the times that you are praying, make sure to forgive anyone that's hurt you, no matter what they've done. Do not walk in unforgiveness towards any of your friends, family, or other people. Forgive so that God, our Father, will also forgive you of your sins.

And when ye stand praying, forgive, if ye have ought against any: that your Father also which is in heaven may forgive you your trespasses.   Mark 11:25

Be patient and forgive one another; even if someone sins against you since Christ forgave you. Forgiveness will keep your fellowship with Jesus open.

Forbearing one another, and forgiving one another, if any man have a quarrel against any: even as Christ forgave you, so also do ye.   Colossians 3:13

If you choose to purposely forgive people when they hurt you, then God will also make sure to forgive you. But, be warned, if you do not forgive them, then God will not forgive you of your sins.

For if ye forgive men their trespasses, your heavenly Father will also forgive you: V. 15 But if ye forgive not men their trespasses, neither will your Father forgive your trespasses.   Matthew 6:14-15

Listen closely; if anyone hurts you, talk to them about it. Forgive them when they apologize to you. God wants us to forgive continually. If that person sins against us seven times in one day, then you are to forgive them seven times in that day as well.

Take heed to yourselves: If thy brother trespass against thee, rebuke him; and if he repent, forgive him. v. 4 And if he trespass against thee seven times in a day, and seven times in a day turn again to thee, saying, I repent; thou shalt forgive him.   Luke 17:3-4

Make sure that you are not a person that stays mad in your heart, is full of rage, angry, or talks evil words saying mean things. Keep all these bad things away from you at all times. God wants you to be nice and compassionate to each other, always ready to forgive because Jesus paid the biggest price of all for us to be forgiven.
Let all bitterness, and wrath, and anger, and clamour, and evil speaking, be put away from you, with all malice: v. 32 And be ye kind one to another, tenderhearted, forgiving one another, even as God for Christ's sake hath forgiven you.   Ephesians 4:31-32

_____

_____

_____

_____

_____

_____

_____

_____

_____

_____

FORGIVENESS TESTIMONY 1

One day I was treated really mean at school by two girls. I tried everything I could to be nice to them so I could be their friend, but they were just not accepting me. Finally, one day they let me be their friend and even let me spend the night. But later I found out they were not the girls I thought they were. They were actually letting me stay overnight just so they could be mean and pick on me. It made me very sad and I felt like nobody cared about me or even knew I was alive. When we saw each other at school the following Monday, they both laughed and made fun of me and told their friends a lot of lies about me. I felt even worse than before and I hated school. The devil was also working on me by lying to me and telling me that I was disgusting, ugly, and poor. Because I chose to believe those girl's lies, as well as that of the devil's, I felt sad all the time and had no confidence in myself. I just wish I would have known about Jesus back then and how much he loves me and thinks I'm the greatest. He loves me so much that he even knows how many hairs are on my head (Luke 12:7) and that I am the apple of his eye (Zechariah 2:8). God is crazy about me and that's all that matters.

Jesus taught me that these kinds of people are not really good friends to hang out with, but we should still pray for them because they may be going through something really hard in their lives. It doesn't mean that we should hang out with them, but they need Jesus too.

FORGIVENESS TESTIMONY 2

Over the years, I've heard about people getting healed after choosing to forgive someone that had deeply hurt them in the past. I've even heard of entire families being put back together after some of them chose to forgive. It's important to always forgive others quickly for things they've done against you or someone you love. It doesn't always mean that you start to hang around them, but you do need to forgive. I know it's not always easy, but we must remember that God forgave us of our sins so we must forgive others of theirs. In fact, the bible says that if you don't forgive others of their sins, he will not forgive you of yours. (Matthew 6:15)

One time I was walking towards my best friend's office and could hear a lot of whispering. I had always thought she cared about me and would never have imagined that she would ever speak evil about me. As I got closer to the office, I heard my name and a curse word so I stopped in my tracks. My best friend and another person I worked with (who was a very bad influence in everyone's lives at the office) were saying horrible lies about me. Tears began to run down my face. Suddenly, I felt God tell me to not go into her office and to just walk away. It was the hardest thing to do because I wanted to defend myself. Instead, I chose to obey the Lord and simply walked away. Later, as my best friend walked into my office area, I stayed silent about everything. I even pretended that nothing had happened. A few weeks later, she overheard that I had known about everything they had said about me.

She was confused and asked why I had kept on talking to her like normal and hadn't confronted her. I told her exactly what I felt God wanted me to do. After she heard this, she said she was very sorry. She cried with me and we hugged. She realized then how powerful forgiveness was.

_____
_____
_____
_____
_____
_____
_____
_____
_____
_____
_____
_____
_____
_____
_____
_____
_____
_____
_____
_____
_____ -
_____
_____

Prayer

Father God, I come to you in the name of Jesus and thank you that your word says that you forgive me of my sins if I forgive others that have sinned against me. After all, Jesus died on the cross to forgive me of my sins. I now know that when I am praying I need to make sure to forgive anyone that's offended me. We also need to forgive before offering any gift to the Lord; such as, singing in the choir or any sort of serving to him. How can we pretend to love the Lord and serve him when we're secretly angry and holding unforgiveness towards someone he died for & loves? Do we really think that you're this dumb & that you don't see our true hearts? Please forgive us for putting you at such a low rank. Regardless of what's happened, we choose to forgive anyone that has hurt our feelings, even if that's people from our very own family. You also tell us to forgive seven times in one day, which really just means that we are to always forgive no matter how many times someone hurts us in that single day.

Please give me the strength to do the right thing and to not hold unforgiveness inside. Please help me to forget all the wrong that has been done to me as well. I know that if I will obey your word, I will be blessed and you will be pleased with me.

In Jesus Name...Amen

Fruit of the Spirit

Fruit of the Spirit

Love – Don't be selfish and always be giving; keeping your mind on love.

Joy – Walk with inner joy no matter what you go through.

Peace – Live with inner peace and extend that peace to others.

Longsuffering – Show mercy, forgiveness, and patience.

Gentleness – Show your light by living life calmly and tenderly.

Goodness – Always be kind and honest, doing good things.

Faith – Have strong confidence in the word, believing it works.

Meekness – Always be humble and submissive towards others.

Temperance – Live a life of self-control & endure with others.

But the Fruit of the Spirit is love,
joy, peace, longsuffering,
gentleness, goodness,
faith, v. 23 Meekness,
temperance: against
such there
is no law.

Galatians 5:22-23

Try and memorize by filling in the blanks without looking:

But the Fruit of the Spirit is:

_____,   _____,

_____,   _____,

_____,   _____,

_____,   _____,

_____: against such there
is no law.   Galatians 5:22-23

Giving

GIVING
When It's Important To give

God tells us to give and to give big so that he can bless us big. He says that if we give, he'll give back to us so much that it'll be like a jar that you fill to the very top with something like sugar. The jar will begin to overflow being pressed down & shaken together. God says that not only he, but people will also give to us this much because if you give a lot, you'll be given a lot back; however, if you give a little, you'll get a little back.

<u>Give, and it shall be given unto you; good measure, pressed down, and shaken together, and running over, shall men give into your bosom. For with the same measure that ye mete withal it shall be measured to you again.</u>   Luke 6:38

Everyone knows that it feels a lot better to bless someone than to receive something. It's fun to get gifts, but God says you are more blessed when you give.

<u>And without all contradiction the less is blessed of the better.</u>   Hebrews 7:7

God wants to challenge you by putting him to the test and releasing back to him his 10% of the money you earn. He wants all your needs to be met, as well as that of your church which is where you should be getting fed the fullness of God's word. He will prove to you that he keeps his word by opening the windows of heaven and giving you huge blessings. (If you get $10, willingly release back to God his $1 because it is holy.)

Bring ye all the tithes into the storehouse, that there may be meat in mine house, and prove me now herewith, saith the Lord of hosts, if I will not open you the windows of heaven, and pour you out a blessing, that there shall not be room enough to receive it.

Malachi 3:10

Always make sure to think about each other's needs and how we can encourage each other. Show your love by doing good things for them like making them dinner or washing the dishes.

And let us consider one another to provoke unto love and to good works.

Hebrews 10:24

God will put in your heart what to give when it comes to offerings or giving to others for different needs like a mission's trip. When God tells you to give, do it with a happy heart because you love to give and not because you have to. God loves when you give cheerfully.

Every man according as he purposeth in his heart, so let him give; not grudgingly, or of necessity: for God loveth a cheerful giver.

1 Corinthians 9:7

If you are the kind of person that is always giving, God says that you will prosper; which means, you will be doing very well in every area of your life. You will be refreshed because you have refreshed others by giving to them during a time they really needed it; such as giving clothes, shoes, food, or even money.

The liberal soul shall be made fat: and he that watereth shall be watered also himself.   Proverbs 11:25

God always wants to bless you with his favor! He does this so that in everything and at all times, you will have all that you need and more; especially, so that you can give abundantly to others like families, missionary's, friends, the homeless, or churches.

And God is able to make all grace abound toward you; that ye, always having all sufficiency in all things, may abound to every good work.   2 Corinthians 9:8

_____

_____

_____

_____

_____

_____

_____

_____

_____

_____

_____

_____

_____

_____

_____

_____

_____

Prayer

Father God, I come to you in the name of Jesus and thank you that your word says that you get so very happy when I give to others. I know it is very important to you. It is also very important that we release back to you what belongs to you; which is the 10% tithe you talk about in Malachi 3:10.

Please help me to always obey your word so that I can be blessed and be able to bless others anytime they need help. I know that giving helps the gospel of Jesus Christ to be spread all over the world. By the way, if I've ever not given when I should have, I ask you to please forgive me. Thank you for giving me a cheerful heart to give.

In Jesus Name...Amen

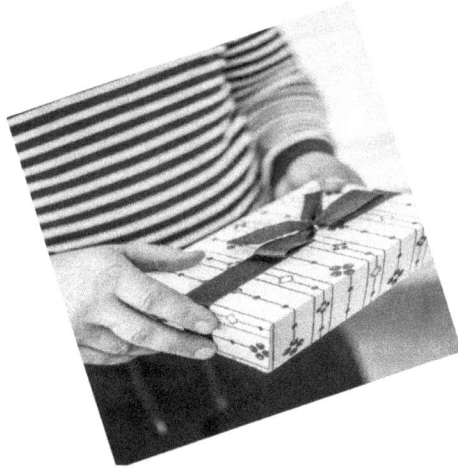

Giving is a good thing to do. It's
a great way to make someone's
day. Jesus gave his whole
life for us. It was
the ultimate
gift.

Ghosts

Ghosts

Are Ghosts Real?

Some people say there are no such things as ghosts, and they're correct. There really are no such things as ghosts. Ghosts are really demons, or as a lot of people call them – evil spirits. They are mean and they all work for the devil. All they want to do is make you sin and think or do bad things to separate you from God's love. Their goal is to steal, kill, and destroy the word of God from you and the plan that God put in your heart to do while you're here on this earth. These evil spirits also want to destroy everything about you and your family. They jump from family to family over many years and try to put the same sicknesses or diseases on one family member that they put on your past families. They are invisible because they are spirits, but sometimes you can see their spirit form, smell, sense, and even hear them. This especially happens when you're not obeying God's word. If you're sinning on purpose, you open the door to these evil spirits to come in and make your life terrible. God can protect you when you stay under the shadow (safety) of his wing, which is his word. It's like a hail storm. If you stay in the house where it's safe, you won't be hurt by the beating of the hail.

The Evil Book...

One day my mother bought a book that talked all about Greek Mythology. It talked about Greek gods and the different kinds of magic they each had. The book had pictures made up of half-men and half-horses. These different gods supposedly gave people different powers. I was really into this book, reading it all the time. There were even words you could repeat out loud called spells that claimed to give you their special powers the more you said them. I began to say them a lot. I was very young but still obsessed over this book.

After a few weeks, I could sense that I had begun to feel different inside. Even though I felt powerful, I also began to feel scared all the time. I seemed to be scared of things that I had never even felt scared about before. The night-time was the worst for me, but I never put two-and-two together. I didn't realize that this book was the reason for all my new fears. Soon, I began to get very interested in scary movies. I couldn't stop watching them and felt so confused. All I knew was that I felt strange and different now. Little did I know that I had just opened the door to the beginning of witchcraft entering into my life.

Slender Man, Charlie–Charlie, Spell Books, Bloody Mary, and Game Boards...

Please don't play games like Slender Man, Charlie-Charlie or etc. They are all tricks of the devil to control you. I know it may seem fake, or sometimes even fun to do with friends, but it is not fake. It is very real. There have been stories of both kids and adults dealing with a lot of bad things after playing with these types of games. And since a lot of them don't know Jesus, they suffer nightmares and attacks.

How to Defeat the Devil

If you ever have a nightmare, or are having bad things happen – cry out to Jesus. He will help you but you must stay away from evil things. Start to say scriptures out loud every day. You should say scriptures and prayers like this:

"In Jesus name, I command you evil spirits to get out of here right now!" because "No weapon formed against me shall prosper!" and "Greater is he that is in me than he that is in the world!" "I repent & renounce all the evil I've allowed into my life and shut the door on all of it, now!"

There are many scriptures in this book that will help you against the enemy. Speak them out loud & be sure to pray, being obedient to the Lord, your parents, and to all those in authority. (1 Timothy 2:1-2)

Read this scripture carefully. It tells you to stay away from evil things and stay close to God. If you do, the devil will have to stay away from you and God will be able to protect you. Repent of your sins, be pure in heart, and not double minded.

Submit yourselves therefore to God. Resist the devil, and he will flee from you. V. 8 Draw nigh to God, and he will draw nigh to you. Cleanse your hands, ye sinners; and purify your hearts, ye double minded.   James 4:7

Was there ever a time you had a bad dream or a scary thing happen to you and you used the name of Jesus to tell it to go away? If you didn't use the name of Jesus, what do you think you'll do the next time you get scared?

_____

_____

_____

_____

_____

_____

_____

_____

_____

_____

_____

_____

_____

_____

_____

God's Love

GOD'S LOVE
When I Need to Know That God Really Loves Me

God loved the people of the world so much that he gave his only son Jesus to die for us. If anyone believes in him, he shall be saved with everlasting life. For God so loved the world, that he gave his only begotten Son, that whosoever believeth in him should not perish, but have everlasting life.   John 3:36

Because you love God, he makes sure that everything works together for good for you. You were called by God to be in his plan. And we know that all things work together for good to them that love God, to them who are the called according to his purpose.   Romans 8:28

God says you are very special to him. He honors and loves you. You are so dear to him that he'd give other people in exchange for you. Since thou wast precious in my sight, thou hast been honourable, and I have loved thee: therefore will I give men for thee, and people for thy life.   Isaiah 43:4

Our Lord is the light of our life & a shield of protection. He gives us favor and never withholds good from us if we continue to obey. For the Lord God is a sun and shield: the Lord will give grace and glory: no good thing will he withhold from them that walk uprightly.

Psalms 84:11

Only good and perfect gifts come from God. He is the father of all light. He shines goodness on us. There is nothing double minded about him. His loving nature never changes.

Every good gift and every perfect gift is from above, and cometh down from the Father of lights, with whom is no variableness, neither shadow of turning.

James 1:17

_____

_____

_____

_____

_____

_____

_____

_____

_____

_____

_____

_____

_____

_____

_____

_____

_____

_____

_____

What kind of things has God done for you that have shown you just how much he loves you?

_____

_____

_____

_____

_____

_____

_____

_____

_____

_____

_____

_____

_____

_____

God's Members

GOD'S MEMBERS
God's Gifts

And God hath set some in the church:

- First **apostles** (In Greek it means: People who are sent for a purpose, like a messenger),
- Secondarily **prophets** (People who speak something important for the future, like a warning that comes straight from God and then tells the message),
- Thirdly **teachers** (People that would teach you the truth about what God's word says),
- After that **miracles** (People that God uses to do heavenly things; like feeding thousands with 5 loaves and 2 fish),
- Then **gifts of healings** (People that God uses a lot to heal other's sicknesses by the power of the Holy Spirit; like healing someone's blind eyes so they can see again),
- **Helps** (People that God uses to help other people, even at church, so that all the work gets done; such as, cleaning, helping people park their cars, saying hello at the front door, singing in the choir, or playing an instrument),
- **Governments** (People who God uses to lead as administrators; giving directions about his word),
- **Diversities of Tongues** (People that God gives an unknown supernatural language to here on earth).

1 Corinthians 12:28

Draw other gifts & color these:

Everyone has different gifts from God so we can all help fulfill his purpose together on earth.

Prayer

Father God, I come to you in the name of Jesus and thank you for all the wonderful gifts you gave to us as your children. I thank you that you have given me a very specific and special gift(s) that you know I will need in order to reach all the people you will put in the path of my life. Thank you for using me to help others not only to be closer to you, but to get saved and give their hearts to you.

Father, I know that the gifts you give me will be very special. Please help me to understand these gifts and show me how I can help others with them. Help me to know what it is you have called me to do in this life so I can start doing them for your kingdom. I know that whatever way you use me, it will help many people in the world.

In Jesus Name...Amen

Gossip

GOSSIP
Talking About Others

A person that hates others is not smart. But a wise person will keep quiet and not gossip.

He that is void of wisdom despiseth his neighbour: but a man of understanding holdeth his peace.

Proverbs 11:12

If you have a fire going but run out of wood, the fire will die out. This is the same way gossip works. If no one keeps the gossip going, then it will die.

Where no wood is, there the fire goeth out: so where there is no talebearer, the strife ceaseth.

Proverbs 26:20

We do many things to hurt people's feelings and we shouldn't, so God says that if we can control the things we say, then we are very smart and mature, and even able to control our very own bodies. **For in many things we offend all. If any man offend not in word, the same is a perfect man, and able also to bridle the whole body.**

James 3:2

When people say mean words to someone, it is like cutting them with a sharp knife. But God says that people that say wise words actually make someone feel better. Kind words bring healing. **There is that speaketh like the piercings of a sword: but the tongue of the wise is health.**   **Proverbs 12:18**

The words you say can either bring life or death to you or someone else. Always remember that you will have to live with the words you speak, so fill them only with words full of life and love.

A wholesome tongue is a tree of life: but perverseness therein is a breach in the spirit.   Proverbs 15:4

_____
_____
_____
_____
_____
_____
_____
_____
_____
_____
_____
_____
_____
_____
_____
_____
_____
_____
_____
_____
_____
_____
_____

Prayer

Father God, I come to you in the name of Jesus and ask you to please help me stop talking about others. I know that gossiping only hurts people's feelings, even my own. I really need your help to keep my mouth quiet. Your word says that even if I listen to the gossip, it's as if I'm gossiping myself because I'm participating in it. I want to act mature and smart by not gossiping or even listening to it. Jesus, I really want to make you proud of me so I thank you for your help.

Also, please forgive me for every time I've started a rumor or even kept one going in the past. It was not nice of me. Forgive me for keeping a gossip going and making fun of others. I know that when things like this have happened to me, it really hurts. Your word says that Jesus didn't even say one word when he was being lied about, beaten, and on his way to Calvary to die for us. So really, we have no excuse. Thank you for helping me to act like Jesus did.

In Jesus Name...Amen

Talking about others may seem interesting
and fun at the time. It may even make you
popular with others just because you
talk about someone with them. But
eventually, that gossip will spread
and really hurt someone's
feelings; especially, if
it's a lie.

Heaven

HEAVEN
My Future Home

Our father God will completely wipe away every single tear from our eyes when we go to heaven. No one will ever have to cry or be sad again. There will be no more death or pain either. All the sadness we are going through now will pass away. Even from our memory. <u>And God shall wipe away all tears from their eyes; and there shall be no more death, neither sorrow, nor crying, neither shall there be any more pain: for the former things are passed away.</u>   Revelation 21:4

God wants us to live by faith. Don't have faith in physical things that may look really bad, but instead keep your eyes on faith. Focus your heart on what is not seen which is spiritual from God in heaven, instead of what is seen. The things of this world are temporary and will end, but the things of God will never end. <u>While we look not at the things which are seen, but at the things which are not seen: for the things which are seen are temporal; but the things which are not seen are eternal.</u>
                    2 Corinthians 4:18

The bible says that in heaven, there's no need for the sun or moon anymore because Jesus is the light of heaven. It will shine so bright that there will be no more night. <u>And the city had no need of the sun, neither of the moon, to shine in it: for the glory of God did lighten it, and the Lamb is the light thereof.</u>   Revelation 21:23

It is very important that you ask Jesus into your heart so that your name can be found in a very big book called, "The Book of Life." This book has all the names of the people that are going to heaven.

And whosoever was not found written in the book of life was cast into the lake of fire.   Revelation 20:15

_____

_____

_____

_____

_____

_____

_____

_____

_____

_____

_____

_____

_____

_____

_____

_____

_____

_____

_____

The bible describes Heaven as the
absolute most beautiful place ever
created. It sounds a lot
like our earth, but way
better. Heaven has
mansions in it
and God has
one there
just for
you.

Heroes of Faith

Heroes of Faith

Abraham and Sarah

Abraham and Sarah were too old to have children and Sarah never was never able to get pregnant while she was young. However, by faith, both Abraham and Sarah put their faith in God's promise and he gave them a baby boy named Isaac. Sarah knew God was faithful to his word. FYI: We are all Abraham's family members too. Whatever promises God gave to him, we get too. <u>Through faith also Sara herself received strength to conceive seed, and was delivered of a child when she was past age, because she judged him faithful who had promised</u>.

Hebrews 11:11

Moses

By faith, when Moses grew up, he refused to worship all the bad gods that the Egyptian people worshipped. He even let everyone know that he didn't want to be called the son of his Egyptian mother anymore. He loved the true God so much that he chose to suffer with his own Israelite people, instead of enjoying all the riches and sins of the Egyptians. He knew the treasures and rewards in God were worth so much more. By faith, Moses even left all he had ever known in Egypt and went into the desert. By faith, he was not afraid of the king of Egypt and stayed strong knowing God was always with him, protecting him, and guiding him and God's people.

<u>By faith Moses, when he was come to years, refused to be called the son of Pharaoh's daughter; V. 25 Choosing rather to suffer affliction with the people of God, than to enjoy the pleasures of sin for a season; V. 26 Esteem-</u>

ing the reproach of Christ greater riches than the treasures in Egypt: for he had respect unto the recompence of the reward. v. 27 By faith he forsook Egypt, not fearing the wrath of the king: for he endured, as seeing him who is invisible.

Hebrews 11:24-27

Enoch

By faith, Enoch who loved God very much, was swooped up and taken up into heaven without ever physically dying. Before he was taken, his testimony before all the people was that he always pleased God because of his faith. It's impossible to please God without it. God rewards those that seek him daily and really want to know him. By faith Enoch was translated that he should not see death; and was not found, because God had translated him: for before his translation he had this testimony, that he pleased God. v. 6 But without faith it is impossible to please him: for he that cometh to God must believe that he is, and that he is a rewarder of them that diligently seek him.   Hebrews 11:5-6

Noah

By faith, Noah built an ark because God told him to. He warned him that a great flood was coming and that everyone would need to stay in the boat in order not to drown. This was God's mercy. He obeyed God and his whole family was saved from the flood. By faith Noah, being warned of God of things not seen as yet, moved with fear, prepared an ark to the saving of his house; by the which he condemned the world, and became heir of the righteousness which is by faith.   Hebrews 11:7

110

Joshua

God spoke to Joshua and told him to march around the city of Jericho that was surrounded by very big walls. After they marched around the city seven times, God told them to shout really, really loud. Joshua and his people shouted (praise) as loud as they could and the walls of Jericho came tumbling down to the ground. God gave all the Israelites the victory because of their very strong faith in him. **By faith the walls of Jericho fell down, after they were compassed about seven days.**

Hebrews 11:30

_____

_____

_____

_____

_____

_____

_____

_____

_____

_____

_____

_____

_____

_____

_____

_____

_____

_____

_____

Holy Spirit

HOLY SPIRIT
He Is Always With Me

The 120 people that were in the upper room where Jesus told them to wait for the Holy Spirit to come began to speak in different languages they hadn't spoken before. The Spirit had come upon them and gave them the power to speak these unknown languages. This amazed all the people outside that spoke some of these languages. They actually thought that the 120 in the upper room had drank too much wine in the morning but Peter told them that they were not drunk with wine or stuff life that, but that they were filled with the Holy Spirit. God was being glorified that day and around 3,000 people were saved and filled with the Spirit, speaking in tongues. <u>And they were all filled with the Holy Ghost, and began to speak with other tongues, as the Spirit gave them utterance.</u>   Acts 2:4

After Jesus had been raised from the dead and just before he was rising back up to heaven, he told them that they would receive power when the Holy Spirit came on them. Because of this power, they would have the boldness and joy of telling others about him; not only in their own cities, but in the surrounding cities, and all over the earth as well. <u>But ye shall receive power, after that the Holy Ghost is come upon you: and ye shall be witnesses unto me both in Jerusalem, and in all Judea, and in Samaria, and unto the uttermost part of the earth.</u>   Acts 1:8

Paul found believers in Ephesus and asked them if they had ever been baptized (filled) with the power of the Holy Spirit. When they said they had never heard of that before, he put his hands on them and 12 of them began to speak in other tongues. They also began to prophesy; which means, they told of things that were going to happen in the future.

And when Paul had laid his hands upon them, the Holy Ghost came on them; and they spake with tongues, and prophesied.   Acts 19:6

God tells us that if you are truly a believer of Jesus, then you will see certain proof follow you. In Jesus name, you will be able to cast out evil spirits from people and speak in new tongues you've never learned before, just by asking the Holy Spirit to fill you. If you accidentally get bit or drink something poisonous, you will not be hurt. Also, you'll be able to put your hands on people and pray for them to be healed and God promises they will be.

And these signs shall follow them that believe; In my name shall they cast out devils; they shall speak with new tongues. V. 15 They shall take up serpents; and if they drink any deadly thing, it shall not hurt them; they shall lay hands on the sick, and they shall recover.   Mark 16:17

When you pray in an unknown heavenly language, you are not speaking to a man or woman, you are speaking directly to God. You will notice that you do not understand what you're praying because you're speaking mysteries by the power of the Holy Spirit. However, you can ask God for the understanding of what you're saying. A lot of times you will hear yourself speaking what you're saying in tongues, in your own language.

For he that speaketh in an unknown tongue speaketh not unto men, but unto God: for no man understandeth him; howbeit in the spirit he speaketh mysteries.

1 Corinthians 14:2

If you speak in these miraculous tongues that even angels speak, but you have no love in your heart, then it means nothing and you're just like a really annoying and loud instrument. Whether we pray in our own understanding or in tongues, it is very important that love is the main reason for praying, since God is love.

Though I speak with the tongues of men and of angels, and have not charity, I am become as sounding brass, or a tinkling cymbal.

1 Corinthians 13:1

_____

_____

_____

_____

_____

_____

_____

_____

_____

_____

_____

_____

Prayer

Father God, I come to you in the name of Jesus and I thank you that before you went back to heaven, you promised to give us power from your Spirit, which is the person named the Holy Spirit. You said that all we had to do was to believe in your son Jesus first, be baptized in water, and then be spiritually baptized by receiving the person of the Holy Spirit to come upon us – filling us within with his power. So because I want to have the full power that you want for me to have in order to walk in your perfect will, live victoriously, and have the boldness to witness to others about you – operating with miracles, signs, and wonders, I ask you to please fill me now with the power of the Holy Spirit, and with the evidence of speaking in tongues. I receive this precious gift, in Jesus name!

Lord, I will now physically open my mouth and allow the heavenly words to come out. I will begin to start praying in my new heavenly "unlearned" language. And though it may sound strange at first, I know that it is coming straight from you. Give me the grace to understand that this is not coming from my head, but from my spirit (since the real me is a spirit being). I freely receive this promised gift by faith and will pray in this new language every day so I can strengthen my faith.

It was God's Holy Spirit that raised Jesus' body from the dead after they had killed him on the cross. So if God's Spirit is living in you, just like he was alive in Jesus, he will also make sure to raise your body and give you life.
But if the Spirit of him that raised up Jesus from the dead dwell in you, he that raised up Christ from the dead shall also quicken your mortal bodies by his Spirit that dwelleth in you.   Romans 8:11

Jealousy

JEALOUSY
When We Feel Jealous

Make sure you stop doing evil things, as well as lying. Don't be a hypocrite telling others to stop doing certain things when there you are doing the same things too. Do not be jealous either. When you're jealous, you start speaking bad things about others. God tells us to get rid of all bad things in our life. It doesn't please him.

Wherefore laying aside all malice, and all guile, and hypocrisies, and envies, and all evil speakings.

1 Peter 2:1

If all you focus on is your bitter jealousies, selfishness, anger, and conceit, then it is wrong. God does not want you boasting and lying. This type of character doesn't come from God, but from the devil.

But if ye have bitter envying and strife in your hearts, glory not, and lie not against the truth. V. 15 This wisdom descendeth not from above, but is earthly, sensual, devilish. James 3:14-15

God wants you to remember that when you are jealous and full of arguing and fighting, you will have a lot of confusion and other very evil things in your life. Stay peaceful and do not be in strife.

For where envying and strife is, there is confusion and every evil work. James 3:16

God says when you have peace in your mind; your body actually stays healthy. But, he says that if you have jealousy in your heart, your bones will actually rot inside you.

A sound heart is the life of the flesh: but envy the rottenness of the bones. Proverbs 14:30

_____
_____
_____
_____
_____
_____
_____
_____
_____
_____
_____
_____
_____
_____
_____
_____
_____
_____
_____
_____
_____
_____
_____

Prayer

Father God, I come to you in the name of Jesus and I thank you for all you've done for me. Your word says that instead of being jealous of other people's things, I should be grateful and thankful for what I already have. Please forgive me for being jealous of people that have things that I don't. Help me to remember to be thankful that they are happy and healthy. I want to always be happy for others, especially when they get an award, lots of money, or do very well in sports. I know that all I have to do is ask you for something I really desire, and if it's your will, and I work hard to get it, I know I will have it because you desire good things for me. I know that anything prayed within your word is always God's will for me.

Thank you for your help, father God. You are so good and so faithful to me.

In Jesus Name...Amen

Love

LOVE
To Be Loved & To Love Others

God tells us that it is very important to love and take care of each other. Jesus says that acting this way helps others know that you are one of his followers because you are kind and show love.

A new commandment I give unto you, That ye love one another; as I have loved you, that ye also love one another. V. 35 By this shall all men know that ye are my disciples, if ye have love one to another.   John 13:34-35

If someone hurts your feelings, make sure to forgive them right away for what they did to you, just like God has forgiven you for all your sins. When you forgive the person that hurt you, they will know that God lives in you and may give their hearts to him too.

And be ye kind one to another, tenderhearted, forgiving one another, even as God for Christ's sake hath forgiven you.   Ephesians 4:32

Make sure to do to others what you would want done to you. Don't be mean. You wouldn't want evil done to you. Instead, do and say nice things because God's law is to love unconditionally.

Therefore all things whatsoever ye would that men should do to you, do ye even so to them: for this is the law and the prophets.   Matthew 7:12

A commandment from the Lord is that we are to love everyone. People that say they love God but hate people, lie. If you love God, then you must also love all the people he created, not just the ones you want to love. **And this commandment have we from him, That he who loveth God love his brother also.**   1 John 4:21

God tells us to love our enemies. I know that can sometimes be hard to do; but with the Lord's strength, we can do it. If someone says something bad about you and is always mean to you, continue to be kind and forgiving towards them so that you will be children of God in heaven. **But I say unto you, Love your enemies, bless them that curse you, do good to them that hate you, and pray for them which despitefully use you, and persecute you; v. 45 That ye may be the children of your Father which is in heaven: for he maketh his sun to rise on the evil and on the good, and sendeth rain on the just and on the unjust.**   Matthew 5:44-55

In this scripture King David said that even though he loved his enemies, they still attacked him. But even after they were so mean to him, he still continued to pray for them. We should do the same. **For my love they are my adversaries: but I give myself unto prayer.**   Psalms 109:4

Let your love be real, not fake. Hate what is evil against God and stay close to what is good. **Let love be without dissimulation. Abhor that which is evil; cleave to that which is good.**   Romans 12:9

124

God loved you so much that he gave us his only son Jesus to come down to the earth and die for us even while we were still sinning. He came to take away all of our sins. God rose Jesus from the dead so that if we would just believe in his son, we could be saved and be with him forever. Nothing can ever separate us from God's love for us and in Him nothing is impossible.

For God so loved the world, that he gave his only begotten Son, that whosoever believeth in him should not perish, but have everlasting life.   John 3:16

_____
_____
_____
_____
_____
_____
_____
_____
_____
_____
_____
_____
_____
_____
_____
_____
_____
_____
_____
_____

1 Corinthians 13:4-7

Charity suffereth long, and is kind; charity envieth not; charity vaunteth not itself, is not puffed up, v. 5 Doth not behave itself unseemly, seeketh not her own, is not easily provoked, thinketh no evil; v. 6 Rejoiceth not in iniquity, but rejoiceth in the truth; v. 7 Beareth all things, believeth all things, hopeth all things, endureth all things.

- o Love is patient and kind:
- o How can you show patience & kindness to someone that has not been very patient or kind to you?

_____

_____

_____

- o Love is not jealous:
- o What can you do to not allow your heart to become jealous or wanting someone else's things?

_____

_____

_____

- o Love does not brag and is not proud:
- o How does God feel about someone always talking about themselves only; always thinking they're better than everyone else God created?

_____

_____

_____

- Love is not rude:
- When was a time that you were rude to someone?

_____
_____
_____

- Love is not selfish:
- How did it feel when someone was selfish with you?

_____
_____
_____

- Love is not easily angered:
- Do you think God gets mad really fast like we do? Why?

_____
_____
_____

- Love holds no record of wrongs:
- Do you think God wants us to remember bad things people did to us? Why?

_____
_____
_____

- Love does not rejoice in evil:
- Should we be happy when someone gets hurt?

_____
_____
_____

Lying

LYING
When I Tell Lies

God tells us to not use our beautiful mouths to tell lies. He also doesn't want us to say things that are mean. They hurt people.

Put away from thee a froward mouth, and perverse lips put far from thee. Proverbs 4:24

Some people love to say curse words and tell all sorts of lies. All they want to talk about is different ways to be mean, cheat, and do bad things. Do not be like them. Be different and walk in love.

His mouth is full of cursing and deceit and fraud: under his tongue is mischief and vanity. Psalms 10:7

God asks you today: Do you really love the life he's given you? And do you really want to be happy in this life he gave you? Then quit saying things to others that hurt them. Don't be mean. Most of all, stop telling lies. Exaggerating is a lie too, so don't do it anymore. Run far from evil and stay in peace as much as possible.

For he that will love life, and see good days, let him refrain his tongue from evil, and his lips that they speak no guile: v. 11 Let him eschew evil, and do good; let him seek peace, and ensue it. 1 Peter 3:10-11

Lies are like sink holes and open pits that swallow us up. God says that lies are like the painful fangs of a snake.

They spill deadly poison into us. Remember, there are no such things as white lies.

Their throat is an open sepulchre; with their tongues they have used deceit; the poison of asps is under their lips. Romans 3:13

Write about a time you lied? What happened because of that lie? Did it hurt you or someone else?

_____

_____

_____

_____

_____

_____

What are some of the things that can happen when you tell a lie?

_____

_____

_____

_____

_____

_____

Prayer

Father God, I come to you in the name of Jesus and I thank you that there's nothing too big for you that you can't forgive. I ask you right now to please forgive me for every time I have ever told a lie. I also repent for all the times I exaggerated something. I know exaggerating means that I blew up a story much bigger than it really was in order to make it sound more dramatic and make people feel sorry for me. Exaggerating is a flat out lie and I apologize very much. I know that lies hurt people and are like the poison from a snake. I will do my best to always tell the truth and be honest.

Thank you for giving me the strength to always obey you by telling others the truth. I know that with you beside me, I can overcome evil with good.

In Jesus Name...Amen

Mourning

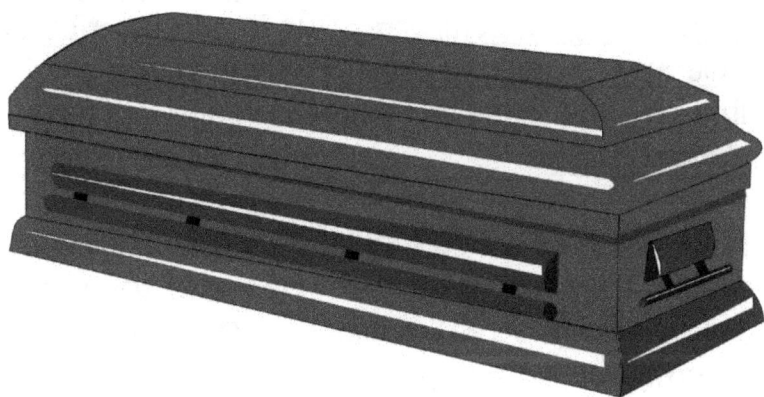

MOURNING
When Someone Dies

Glory to God the Father of our precious Lord Jesus Christ who is the Father of all kindness and a God that loves to comfort and hold us in his arms when we are sad or hurting. He is the God that helps us feel better when we have lost someone through death. He also helps us when we go through hard things in our life. He comforts us so that we can also comfort others through their hard times with this same relief.

Blessed be God, even the Father of our Lord Jesus Christ, the Father of mercies, and the God of all comfort; v. 4 Who comforteth us in all our tribulation, that we may be able to comfort them which are in any trouble, by the comfort wherewith we ourselves are comforted of God.   2 Corinthians 1:3-4

God's words to us are so special that they bring peace to those who have lost their way and are in total sadness. His words give us strength when we feel we just cannot stand anymore. He is so good.

Thy words have upholden him that was falling, and thou has strengthened the feeble knees.   Job 4:4

Even if I have to go through the hardest time of my life, I know that I don't have to go through it alone or be afraid because the Lord is always with me. Like a shepherd directs, guides, and cares for his sheep, God will do the same for me and anyone who trusts in him.

Yea, though I walk through the valley of the shadow of death, I will fear no evil: for thou art with me; thy rod and thy staff they comfort me.   Psalms 23:4

If someone is happy, be happy with them. But if someone is sad, be there for them so they can be comforted and know you care.

Rejoice with them that do rejoice, and weep with them that weep.   Romans 12:15

_____

_____

_____

_____

_____

_____

_____

_____

_____

_____

_____

_____

_____

_____

_____

_____

_____

_____

_____

_____

_____

_____

It's very hard to lose a friend, family member, or even a pet. God can help to heal your heart from the sadness. Trust in him because he cares for you. He takes all the heaviness and brings you joy.

Prayer

Father God, I come to you in the name of Jesus. I just want to tell you that I am so very sad. I really need you right now like I've never needed you before. You already know how special this person was to me that died. I am feeling so lonely without them and I feel like I can't ever get through this. Help me to understand what you felt in your heart when you watched your only son Jesus die on the cross for the sins of the whole world.

Lord, please give me the strength to get through this. I know that you can give me your peace that passes all understanding. Help me to know that I will see them again in heaven. Thank you for healing my heart by being the God of all comfort.

In Jesus Name...Amen

Nicodemus

NICODEMUS

Have you ever been afraid to show others that you believe in Jesus because you might be made fun of or get into trouble? We should never be ashamed to let others know of Jesus' love for them.

The bible tells us that there was a man named Nicodemus. He lived in Jerusalem. He was a Pharisee and a very important Jewish leader. He came to Jesus at night. He probably didn't want others who didn't believe in him to see him asking Jesus questions. The same came to Jesus by night, and said unto him, Rabbi we know that thou art a teacher come from God: for no man can do these miracles that thou doest, except God be with him. V. 3 Jesus answered and said unto him, Verily, verily, I say unto thee, Except a man be born again, he cannot see the kingdom of God. V. 4 Nicodemus saith unto him, How can a man be born when he is old? Can he enter the second time into this mother's womb, and be born? V. 5 Jesus answered, Verily, verily, I say unto thee, Except a man be born of water and of the Spirit, he cannot enter into the kingdom of God. V. 6 That which is born of the flesh is flesh; and that which is born of the Spirit is spirit. V. 7 Marvel not that I said unto thee, Ye must be born again.   John 3:2-7

Jesus told Nicodemus a very important scripture: For God so loved the world, that he gave his only begotten Son, that whosoever believeth in him should not perish, but have everlasting life.   John 3:16

Obedience

OBEDIENCE
When I Make Good & Bad Choices

Make sure to always obey your parents. This is right in the eyes of the Lord. He wants you to honor them by respecting them and doing the things they tell you to do, as well as not doing the things they tell you not to do. This is the Lord's 1st command to us that comes with a promise attached to it. Do this and it will be well with you. Plus, you'll end up living a long life on the earth.

Children, obey your parents in the Lord: for this is right. V. 2 Honour thy father and mother; (which is the first commandment with promise;) V. 3 That it may be well with thee, and thou mayest live long on the earth.

Ephesians 6:1-3

Children that act evil against their parents; disobeying, cursing, and being disrespectful on purpose, will have the light of their life cut short and put in darkness.

Whoso curseth his father or his mother, his lamp shall be put out in obscure darkness.   **Proverbs 20:20**

God wants our love for others to grow more and more so that we will learn to do good things with this love. If we do this, we will also be able to know the difference between what is good and what is bad; choosing good and pure things. We'll also be able to make the right choices and be found obedient when Jesus comes to take us home.

And this I pray, that your love may abound yet more and more in knowledge and in all judgment; v. 10 That ye may approve things that are excellent; that ye may be sincere and without offence till the day of Christ.

Philippians 1:9-10

Obey those that have authority over you. Make sure to do what they say by being respectful and obedient because they watch over you to make sure you're always okay. One day they will have to tell God how they took care of you, so make their hearts happy and not full of heartache. This is what's best for you anyway.

Obey them that have the rule over you, and submit yourselves: for they watch for your souls, as they that must give account, that they may do it with joy, and not with grief: for that is unprofitable for you.

Hebrews 13:17

_____
_____
_____
_____
_____
_____
_____
_____
_____
_____
_____
_____
_____
_____

Prayer

Father God, I come to you in the name of Jesus and ask you to please forgive me for disobeying my parents, teachers, and all those in authority over me. Your word is very clear when it says that if we disobey our parents, the light of our life on earth could be cut short. I can see this happening because we could really get ourselves in dangerous trouble; especially, if we disobey the laws of our country. I'm glad, though, that your word says that if we will obey our parents, we will have a long life here on this earth.

Please give me the strength to always be obedient and respectful to everyone, even to my friends because I know they are gifts from you. Thank you for forgiving me. I love you.

In Jesus Name...Amen

What are some examples of obedience?

1. _____

_____

_____

_____

_____

2. _____

_____

_____

_____

_____

3. _____

_____

_____

_____

_____

Draw other pictures of obedience:

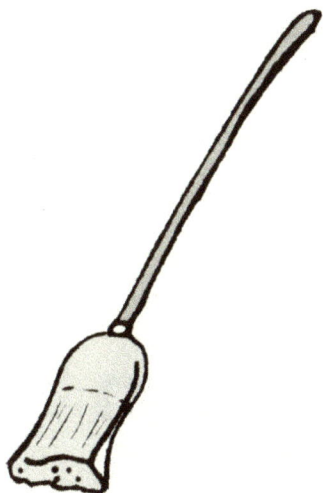

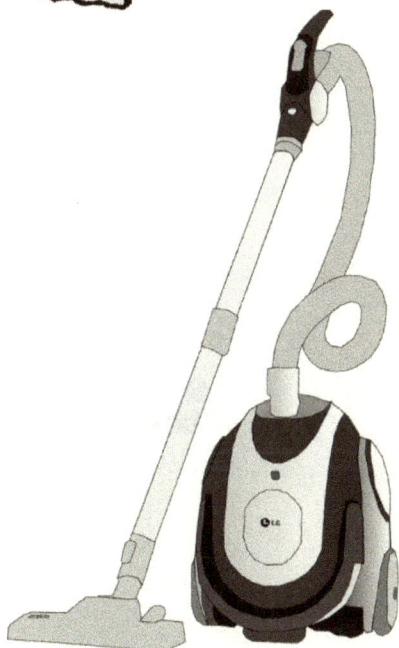

Offense

OFFENSE
When Someone Insults Me

I'll be okay when I go through hard times like people insulting me, sufferings, being made fun of, or other tough things because I know it's all for the sake of Christ. When I feel weak in my own strength, I know I'm actually strong through God's power. <u>Therefore I take pleasure in infirmities, in reproaches, in necessities, in persecutions, in distresses for Christ's sake: for when I am weak, then am I strong.</u>   2 Corinthians 12:10

God calls you blessed when you stand strong against temptations like getting offended, angry, or sinning. When you stand strong until the end, you will receive the gift of eternal life. <u>Blessed is the man that endureth temptation: for when he is tried, he shall receive the crown of life, which the Lord hath promised to them that love him.</u>   James 1:12

Stay wide awake and on guard because your enemy, the devil, walks around like a very loud lion, looking for any one he can destroy. <u>Be sober, be vigilant; because your adversary the devil, as a roaring lion, walketh about, seeking whom he may devour.</u>   1 Peter 5:8

Be quick to hear, slow to speak, and slow to anger. <u>Wherefore, my beloved brethren, let every man be swift to hear, slow to speak, slow to wrath.</u>   James 1:19

The careful person watches over their mouth and stays both quiet & calm. It is a person's mature status & honor to forgive when something wrong is said or done to them. <u>The discretion of a man deferreth his anger; and it is his glory to pass over a transgression.</u>   Proverbs 19:11

_____
_____
_____
_____
_____
_____
_____
_____
_____
_____
_____
_____
_____
_____
_____
_____
_____
_____
_____
_____
_____

Prayer

Father God, I come to you in the name of Jesus and thank you that you always give us the strength to overcome feelings of pain and hurt. It really feels terrible when people make rude comments, disrespect us, talk about us, belittle us, and give us dirty looks. It feels awful and makes me feel like I'm not important at all. But I thank you that I am very important to you. And if people did all these evil things to Jesus, then I count it all joy when I go through the same things Jesus went through.

Right now, I choose to forgive this offense and the person(s) that hurt me. I thank you for the strength to be strong and to not fall into the trap of the enemy. I know that we have a chance to get offended every single day, but I also know that with the strength of your word, I can walk away, stay calm, and trust in you.

In Jesus Name...Amen

What are some things you can do or say to not get offended? Maybe saying a scripture or walking away?

1. _____
_____
_____
_____
_____
_____

2. _____
_____
_____
_____
_____
_____

3. _____
_____
_____
_____
_____
_____

Don't ever be rude or say things you shouldn't. Though that person may not seem like it bothers them, I can assure you it does. It can really hurt someone's feelings. Sometimes even for a life-time.

Prayer

PRAYER
Importance of a Prayer Life

The bible tells us to always have a life that includes prayer with it. It also tells us that it is actually God's will for us to always be thankful to him for all that we have. **Pray without ceasing. In everything give thanks: for this is the will of God in Christ Jesus concerning you.**

1 Thessalonians 5:17-18

Our Lord is very near to everyone who calls out and prays to him sincerely from deep within their heart. **The Lord is nigh unto all them that call upon him, to all that call upon him in truth.** Psalms 145:18

It's important to God that you spend time with him. He asks us to go into our rooms or closets and shut the door so that the two of you can spend alone time together. The Lord can see you in this secret place with him and will reward you in front of others. And though you can't see him looking at you, he can see & hear you. **But thou, when thou prayest, enter into thy closet, and when thou hast shut thy door, pray to thy Father which is in secret; and thy Father which seeth in secret shall reward thee openly.** Matthew 6:6

If someone is having a very hard time in their life, they should pray. If any are happy, they should sing songs of praise. **Is any among you afflicted? let him pray. Is any merry? let him sing Psalms.** James 5:13

God tells us to come to him without any fear during the times that we feel down and afraid. He wants us to come to him boldly to his throne of grace so we can be empowered by him. We can do this because of Jesus' blood that was shed on Calvary for us. It is a privilege to be able to pray to our Holy God. When we pray to him, we can expect to find his mercy, power, and favor for us.

Let us therefore come boldly unto the throne of grace, that we may obtain mercy, and find grace to help in time of need. Hebrews 4:16

Jesus told his disciples (and to us) to pray that God's desires would be done here on earth as it is in heaven. That what God desires to be fulfilled on the earth; such as, healing, deliverance, mercy, love, joy, prosperity, and peace would be fulfilled. This is what God wants for us here on earth, just like it is in heaven.

Thy kingdom come. Thy will be done in earth, as it is in heaven. Matthew 6:10

When you pray, don't pray in front of others really loud or just to be seen so that people think you are better than they are. These kinds of people will not be heard because they are only praying to show off and that will be their only reward. God doesn't mind if you pray in prayer groups or at church or wherever, just make sure you're praying from a true heart. Not a fake one.

And when thou prayest, thou shalt not be as the hypocrites are: for they love to pray standing in the synagogues and in the corners of the streets, that they may be seen of men. Verily I say unto you, they have their reward. Matthew 6:5

God tells us to always pray for the peace of Jerusalem and its entire people. The Jews are the people that Jesus came from and God's holy people. Those that love Jerusalem shall do well & be safe.

Pray for the peace of Jerusalem: they shall prosper that love thee. Psalms 122:6

One day Jesus was praying to his Father God that all people that believe in him would become one with them. He wants everyone to know that he is in God and God is in him. He wants the world to know this so that they can believe that he was sent by God himself.

That they all may be one; as thou, Father, art in me, and I in thee, that they also may be one in us: that the world may believe that thou hast sent me. John 17:21

Always pray in the Spirit and all the time with different kinds of prayers; thankful prayers, prayers for help, and even prayers of need. Pray with strength and patience – never giving up praying for God's people.

Praying always with all prayer and supplication in the Spirit, and watching thereunto with all perseverance and supplication for all saints. Ephesians 6:18

God wants you to know that if you pray according to his word and don't doubt what you have prayed will come to pass; then he'll give you the desires of your heart. Always remember that your desire must be a good one that you know God's word would approve of. But, when you start praying about whatever it is you need or want, make sure that you have forgiven anyone that has hurt your feelings so that God can answer your prayers and forgive you of your sins.

For verily I say unto you, That whosoever shall say unto this mountain, Be thou removed, and be thou cast into the sea; and shall not doubt in his heart, but shall believe that those things which he saith shall come to pass; he shall have whatsoever he saith. v. 24 Therefore I say unto you, What things soever ye desire, when ye pray, believe that ye receive them, and ye shall have them. v. 25 And when ye stand praying, forgive, if ye have ought against any: that your Father also which is in heaven may forgive you your trespasses: v. 26 But if ye do not forgive, neither will your Father which is in heaven forgive your trespasses.   Mark 11:23-26

EMPTY WORDS...EMPTY PRAYERS

Some religions teach their church members to say the same type of meaningless prayers over and over again. But the bible clearly tells us that when we pray, we are not to use prayers that repeat the same words over and over again. The bible describes them as worth nothing. Don't do what the world does when they say repetitious prayers. These people think that they're being heard by God but they are not being heard at all. God wants us to pray from our hearts as a friend to him because he is not only our God, but he is our faithful friend.

But when ye pray, use not vain repetitions, as the heathen do: for they think that they shall be heard for their much speaking. Matthew 6:7

How would it make you feel if your family or friends said the same exact thing to you every time they saw you?
++

_____

_____

_____

_____

_____

_____

_____

_____

_____

_____

_____

_____

_____

First day: "_____, I need your help so please do what I asked you to do for me, thanks."

Later that day: "_____, I need your help so please do what I asked you to do for me, thanks."

Next day: "_____, I need your help so please do what I asked you to do for me, thanks?

Day after that: "_____, I need your help so please do what I asked you to do for me, thanks."

Next week: "_____, I need your help so please do what I asked you to do for me, thanks."

- Do you think there's much of a friendship here?

- Wouldn't it be weird to hear someone say the same thing to you every time they saw you, even if you were just going to bed or to eat dinner?

- This is how God feels. Unloved by empty words.

- He doesn't want empty words.

- He wants to hear words that come from your heart.

- He wants them to be real and to show what you are really feeling inside.

Preaching

PREACHING
Telling People about Jesus

God loved the people he created in the world so much that he sent his only son Jesus to come into the world and die for everyone that had sinned. If you will believe in him, you will have eternity forever.

For God so loved the world, that he gave his only begotten Son, that whosoever believeth in him should not perish, but have everlasting life.   John 3:16

Jesus told us all to go into the whole world and preach the gospel to every single person we meet.

And he said unto them, Go ye into all the world, and preach the gospel to every creature.   Mark 16:15

Tell people that God's kingdom is coming very soon. God also tells us to lay our hands on sick people and pray for them to be healed in Jesus' name. He wants us to raise dead people up and also command demons to come out of people. God gave us this authority but only through Jesus' name. We are his vessels to be used by him. His power goes through us as we pray in his son's name. God freed us of sin and many other things, so we should also freely pray for others.

And as ye go, preach, saying, The kingdom of heaven is at hand. v. 8 Heal the sick, cleanse the lepers, raise the dead, cast out devils: freely ye have received, freely give. Matthew 10:7-8

When you preach to people about Jesus, make sure you are graceful and hold their attention. Be careful what words you choose to say to them. Make sure to study God's word every day so you can answer as many questions as you can that unbelievers may ask you.

Let your speech be always with grace, seasoned with salt, that ye may know how ye ought to answer every man.   Colossians 4:6

The Spirit of God is in you. He has chosen you to preach the good news to everyone. He sends you to preach so that you can tell all the people of the world that are a slave to the devil that they can be free. He wants you to tell the blind that they can see again and those that are hurting that they are healed in their minds & bodies.

The Spirit of the Lord is upon me, because he hath anointed me to preach the gospel to the poor; he hath sent me to heal the brokenhearted, to preach deliverance to the captives, and recovering of sight to the blind, to set at liberty them are bruised.   Luke 4:18

The apostle Paul was telling the Ephesians that since God made him a minister of the word of God, by putting his gift of power inside him, it has become his wonderful job to spread the good news of the gospel to every person he meets.

Whereof I was made a minister, according to the gift of the grace of God given unto me by the effectual working of his power.   Ephesians 3:7

Studying God's word gives you God's approval so you can tell the world about the true gospel; not giving the wrong meanings about his scriptures and messages. Reading the bible everyday will help you understand and show others exactly what God wants you to tell them. Also, you will never be tricked into believing the words of people that try to teach you something that is not true about the bible. They are false teachers. Stay away from them.

Study to shew thyself approved unto God, a workman that needeth not to be ashamed, rightly dividing the word of truth.   2 Timothy 2:15

_____
_____
_____
_____
_____
_____
_____
_____
_____
_____
_____
_____
_____
_____
_____
_____
_____
_____

We should always share the good news to everyone we meet. They deserve to hear about how much God loves them, too. God will give us the boldness and wisdom to know what to say to them. Make sure to be a good example as well. This will give God the glory.

Prayer

Father God, I come to you in the name of Jesus and thank you so very much for sending Jesus to die for us. I know that he didn't just die for our sins and eternity, but he also took away all of our sicknesses and diseases, then gave us power to fulfill everything he called us to do on this earth through the power of the Holy Spirit.

I ask that you would please give me the strength and power to speak your word and gospel to others boldly and without fear. Help me to say exactly what you want me to say to each person you put before me. Bring people to me that need you.

In Jesus Name...Amen

What are some of the things you can say to tell others about Jesus? What scriptures can you use?

1. _____
_____
_____
_____

2. _____
_____
_____
_____

3. _____
_____
_____
_____

4. _____
_____
_____
_____

5. _____
_____
_____
_____

6. _____
_____
_____
_____

Protection

PROTECTION
When I Need Protection

I speak to my soul which is my mind, will, and emotions; telling you to trust and wait on the Lord for what you need since he is your hope. God is also your firm foundation and salvation. He is your defender; therefore, trust in him with all your heart, regardless of what you see, and then you will never be moved in fear.

My soul, wait thou only upon God; for my expectation is from him. v. 6 He only is my rock and my salvation: he is my defence; I shall not be moved.   **Psalms 62:5-6**

It's much smarter to trust the Lord with every area of your life than to put your trust in a friend or even a family member. God will never fail you but a person eventually will.

It is better to trust in the Lord than to put confidence in man.   **Psalms 118:8**

Hear my prayer, Lord. Consider my time with you as precious. Hear my cry, my king, and my God. To you will I always pray and my voice you will always hear in the morning. Lord, in the morning I will talk with you and will look up towards the heavens for you are my God.

Give ear to my words, O Lord, consider my meditation. v. 2 Hearken unto the voice of my cry, my King, and my God: for unto thee will I pray. v. 3 My voice shalt thou hear in the morning, O Lord; in the morning will I direct my prayer unto thee, and will look up.   **Psalms 5:1-3**

The Lord will bless those that walk in his ways. They will have favor, be protected, and surrounded like a shield.
For thou, Lord, wilt bless the righteous; with favour will thou compass him as with a shield.   Psalms 5:12

There will be many trials during your walk with Jesus because the devil does everything he can to put them on you. There are also many troubles because we live in a world that does not obey God. However, the Lord will deliver you out of every single issue if you will just put your complete trust and confidence in him.
Many are the afflictions of the righteous: but the Lord delivereth him out of them all.   Psalms 34:19

God is always our shelter and strength. If we are in trouble, he will be there to help us.
God is our refuge and strength, a very present help in trouble.   Psalms 46:1

When all my enemies surround me, deliver me like you say you will, dear God. Defend me from all that attack me.
Deliver me from mine enemies, O my God: defend me from them that rise up against me.   Psalms 59:1

Be very sure of your faith and courage in the Lord. Do not fear anything, or anyone that comes against you because the Lord your God is always going with you and will not fail to protect you. He will never disown you or abandon you.

Be strong and of a good courage, fear not, nor be afraid
of them: for the Lord thy God, he it is that doth go
with thee; he will not fail thee, nor forsake thee.
                                          Deuteronomy 31:6

I will remember to lift up my eyes to the Lord that made
heaven and earth because this is where my help comes
from and will always come from. He won't let me stumble
because he is the one that watches over me; never
falling asleep, but always keeping watch.
I will lift up mine eyes unto the hills, from whence
cometh my help. V. 2 My help cometh from the Lord,
which made heaven and earth. V. 3 He will not suffer thy
foot to be moved: he that keepeth thee will not
slumber.   Psalms 121:1-3

_____
_____
_____
_____
_____
_____
_____
_____
_____
_____
_____
_____
_____
_____
_____
_____
_____

Protection Testimony

My name is Brian. I am a Journeyman Lineman. That means that I repair power lines that stop working. It is a very important job that took several years of apprenticeship school to learn. There are many reasons we need power in our communities. One of them is so you can stay warm during the winter or cool during the summer. Many places like hospitals need power to take care of sick people because of the machines they use. You even need power to go to school because of computers and lights. It would be hard to learn in the dark (though it might be a little fun at first☺). Sometimes, I'm sent far away from my family for a long time to other states in order to repair power lines that have fallen or have become broken during hurricanes, ice storms, or tornadoes. Overall, my job is a very important job; however, it is also a very dangerous job. You don't really get second chances if you accidentally touch a power line that is charged with electricity. Here's my story of God's protection on me.

One day I was rebuilding an overhead power line that I was converting to an underground power line. As usual, I had prayed that morning for God's protection over me. As I was working, I made a mistake and my armor rod (wire) touched a bolt that was touching the ground being charged with electricity. Immediately, I caused what we call an "arc flash" to occur. The power from this kind of flash can bring immediate death because it puts out extreme heat that is about 10 times hotter than the sun. As the arc flash occurred; suddenly, I saw a misty-black object that looked like some sort of round orb hover right over the power coming from the flash. I could actually see the very bright arc flash behind this orb. The orb then stayed between the arc flash and my body for a few seconds, enough for me to get to safety. The hair on my chin and head got burned, but my face and everything else had been saved. I knew that either an angel or the Lord himself had put his hand there to block the arc flash from harming me; otherwise, I may not have been here to tell you this story today. Thank you, Jesus!

Prayer

Father God, I come to you in the name of Jesus. I thank you so much for always protecting us. Your word says that you always watch over us to make sure that we're taken care of. We know that you also have your holy angels charge over us to keep us in all our ways.

Lord I ask that you please help me to always have faith and know that you are with me, as well as with all those around me that I love. I choose to trust you with my whole life. Even with the purpose you made me for. I thank you that your word says that no weapon formed against me shall prosper. I believe your words and thank you that you satisfy me with long life because I follow your ways.

In Jesus Name...Amen

God has set his angels in charge over you
to protect you and keep you safe. It
is God's will for you to be healthy
and to live a long life. Obey
his word so that you will
stay safe and not be an
easy target for
the devil.

Psalms 23

The LORD is my shepherd; I shall not want. v. 2 He maketh me to lie down in green pastures: he leadeth me beside the still waters. v. 3 He restoreth my soul: he leadeth me in the paths of righteousness for his name's sake. v. 4 Yea, though I walk through the valley of the shadow of death, I will fear no evil: for thou art with me; thy rod and thy staff they comfort me. v. 5 Thou preparest a table before me in the presence of mine enemies: thou anointest my head with oil; my cup runneth over. v. 6 Surely goodness and mercy shall follow me all the days of my life: and I will dwell in the house of the LORD forever.

Psalms 91
(Put your name in the blank of this prayer)

I, _____ that dwelleth in the secret place of the most High shall abide under the shadow of the Almighty. v. 2 I, _____ will say of the Lord, He is my refuge and my fortress: my God; in him will I trust. v. 3 Surely he shall deliver _____ from the snare of the fowler, and from the noisome pestilence. v. 4 He shall cover _____ with his feathers, and under his wings shalt thou trust: his truth shall be thy shield and buckler. v. 5 _____ shalt not be afraid for the terror by night; nor for the arrow that flieth by day; v. 6 Nor for the pestilence that walketh in darkness; nor for the destruction that wasteth at noonday. v. 7 A thousand shall fall at _____ side, and the thousand at thy right hand; but it shall not come nigh _____. v. 8 Only with thine eyes shalt thou behold and see the reward of the wicked. v. 9 Because _____ hast made the Lord, which is my refuge, even the most High, thy habitation; v. 10 There shall no evil befall _____, neither shall any plague come nigh _____ dwelling. V. 11 For he shall give his angels charge over _____, to keep thee in all thy ways. V. 12 They shall bear _____ up in their hands, lest thou dash thy foot against a stone. V. 13 Thou shalt tread upon the lion and adder: the young lion and dragon shalt thou trample under feet. V. 14 Because _____ hath set his love upon me, therefore will I deliver him: I will set _____ on high, because _____ hath known my name. V. 15 _____ shall call upon me, and I will answer _____: I will be with _____ in trouble; I will deliver _____, and honour him. V. 16 With long life will I satisfy _____, and shew _____ my salvation.

Sadness

SADNESS
When I Feel Depressed

Why are you sad, soul inside me? And why are you worried and full of anxiety? Put your trust in God and praise him. He's the one that makes us feel better and lifts our joy. He is our God.

<u>Why are thou cast down, O my soul? and why art thou disquieted within me? hope thou in God: for I shall yet praise him, who is the health of my countenance, and my God.</u>   Psalms 42:11

I bless our God; the God and Father of our Lord Jesus Christ who is the Father of mercies and comfort. He puts calmness and peace in our hearts when we go through hard times so that we can bring calmness and peace to others that are having troubles too.

<u>Blessed be God, even the Father of our Lord Jesus Christ, the Father of mercies, and the God of all comfort; v. 4 Who comforteth us in all our tribulation, that we may be able to comfort them which are in any trouble, by the comfort wherewith we ourselves are comforted of God.</u>   2 Corinthians 1:3-4

Every day is a new day that the Lord has made just for us. It is also an opportunity to live our life joyful through obedience; therefore, let us do all we can to rejoice and be happy, stirring up joy every moment.

<u>This is the day which the Lord hath made; we will rejoice and be glad in it.</u>   Psalms 118:24

God has spoken to us words of comfort through his scriptures so that we can have the peace that passes all understanding in a world that is full of sadness & suffering. Be cheerful knowing that God has given us the keys to overcome life's hard times and live in victory. These things I have spoken unto you, that in me ye might have peace. In the world ye shall have tribulation: but be of good cheer; I have overcome the world.

John 16:33

Even though I was so sad, I waited patiently for the Lord. He heard my prayer and even my cries to him. I was in such despair of sadness but he brought me out of this horrible pit I was in; out of my mud pit where I felt stuck. He then put my feet way up high on a rock so that I was no longer sad and low, stuck in the mud. He has helped me live on and has even put a happy song in my heart so I now praise him. Lots of people will see how God has helped me and will respect him and begin to trust in him like I did.

I waited patiently for the Lord; and he inclined unto me, and heard my cry. V. 2 He brought me up also out of an horrible pit, out of the miry clay, and set my feet upon a rock, and established my goings. V. 3 And he hath put a new song in my mouth, even praise unto our God: many shall see it, and fear, and shall trust in the Lord.

Psalms 40:1-3

We are absolutely sure that not death, life, angels, demons, nor powers, nor things going on now or to come; nor height, nor the deep, nor any creature, shall ever be able to separate us from the love that God has for us which is in Christ Jesus our Lord.

For I am persuaded, that neither death, nor life, nor angels, nor principalities, nor powers, nor things present, nor things to come, v. 39 Nor height, nor depth, nor any other creature, shall be able to separate us from the love of God, which is in Christ Jesus our Lord.

Romans 8:38-39

People of God; remember to think only about things that are truthful and honest, holy and pure, with good news, of worth, and praiseworthy unto the Lord. Only think on these things.

Finally, brethren, whatsoever things are true, whatsoever things are honest, whatsoever things are just, whatsoever things are pure, whatsoever things are lovely, whatsoever things are of good report; if there be any virtue, and if there be any praise, think on these things.

Philippians 4:8

_____
_____
_____
_____
_____
_____
_____
_____
_____
_____
_____
_____
_____
_____
_____

Prayer

Father God, I come to you in the name of Jesus. I know that you already know how sad I am and that I really need you today. Sometimes people are sad for different reasons; like someone hurting their feelings or making fun of them. Maybe others are sad because someone they love may have died. I know that some of my friends get sad when their parents get into a fight; especially, if they're going through a divorce or have gotten one. Please help us to know that no matter what happens in our lives, your word says that you're the God of all comfort and peace. You're always there with us.

Father God, please fill my heart with that peace that can only come from you. I need your strength to fill me right now. I'm going through a really hard time in my life and really need you. No one understands how bad my heart hurts like you do. Please give me the strength to be happy again. I rebuke the spirit of depression from me and know that this too shall pass.

In Jesus Name...Amen

Salvation

SALVATION
Saved and Forgiven

Go into the entire world, and especially to the areas around you, and preach the good news of Jesus to every single person you meet. The person that believes your message will be saved. But if they don't believe, then they will spend eternity without him because of their own choice. God will never force them to follow him. He wants them to follow because of love.

<u>And he said unto them, Go ye into all the world, and preach the gospel to every creature. v. 16 He that believeth and is baptized shall be saved; but he that believeth not shall be damned.</u>   Mark 16:15-16

God says that if you are truly a believer, then signs will follow you. In Jesus name you will command evil spirits to leave and they have to obey. Believers will speak with new tongues by praying in the Holy Spirit and being baptized by him. If they accidentally get bit by a creature that is harmful, they will not die. Even if they accidentally drink something that can kill them, it will not hurt them. When they pray for people & lay their hands on their bodies, they will be healed.

<u>And these signs shall follow them that believe; In my name shall they cast out devils; they shall speak with new tongues; v. 18 They shall take up serpents; and if they drink any deadly thing, it shall not hurt them; they shall lay hands on the sick, and they shall recover.</u>
Mark 16:17-18

Whoever believes in Jesus will have everlasting life with him. But he that chooses not to believe in Jesus will not see this life or be able to be with him for eternity.

He that believeth on the Son hath everlasting life: and he that believeth not the Son shall not see life; but the wrath of God abideth on him.   John 3:36

It's only by God's gift of grace and empowerment by the Holy Spirit (not by any wonderful works we've ever done that we need to show off about) that we are saved. It is only through Jesus Christ's gracious sacrifice on the cross. We are God's workers, created in Christ Jesus for good works. God already anointed us so that we can do these good works for the gospel.

For by grace are ye saved through faith; and that not of yourselves: it is the gift of God: v. 9 Not of works, lest any man should boast. v. 10 For we are his workmanship, created in Christ Jesus unto good works, which God hath before ordained that we should walk in them.
                                        Ephesians 2:8-9

If we ask God to forgive us of all of our sins, he is true to his word and will forgive us if we truly repent. He will make us clean in our spirit from all the bad we've done.

If we confess our sins, he is faithful and just to forgive us our sins, and to cleanse us from all unrighteousness.
                                              1 John 1:9

Paul and Silas told the people to believe in the Lord Jesus Christ and then they could be saved, even everyone in their family.

And they said, Believe on the Lord Jesus Christ, and thou shalt be saved, and thy house. Acts 16:31

With everything in my heart, I wait on the Lord my God because it is in him that I have all that I need; including, my salvation. He is my rock and my deliverer. He is also my defender. I will not be moved!
Truly my soul waiteth upon God: from him cometh my salvation. v. 2 He only is my rock and my salvation; he is my defence; I shall not be greatly moved.
Psalms 62:1-2

God sent us his Holy Spirit through Jesus Christ our Savior.
Which he shed on us abundantly through Jesus Christ our Savior. Titus 3:6

_____
_____
_____
_____
_____
_____
_____
_____
_____
_____
_____
_____
_____
_____
_____
_____

Prayer

Father God, I come to you by faith in the name of Jesus that you say is the only name in which any person can be saved. Your word says that if we would just believe and confess our sins to you, you would forgive us. I ask you to please forgive me for every bad thing I've ever done in my life up to now. I truly repent. I've learned that the word "repent" means that we are to do our best to turn away from sin and not do it on purpose any more. I also repent for not appreciating you and ignoring your salvation and goodness for me all these years. Jesus, please come into my heart and be my savior and Lord. I don't just want you to save me from eternity without you, but I want you to be the Lord over every part of my life. I believe & confess that you came to this earth, died for us, and then rose again – sending down the Holy Spirit for us. Please fill me with your Holy Spirit so I can have the power and boldness I need to be strong in my Christian walk.

Thank you that I am now born-again by your Holy Spirit and that I am a new person in Christ. The old me has passed away and I am now filled with the newness of life. Help me to live by Romans 12:2 that tells us to always renew our minds to the word of God.

In Jesus Name...Amen

No one will ever be able to find salvation
in any other name under heaven that has
been given to men, where they can be
saved. <u>Neither is there salvation
in any other: for there is no
other name under heaven
given among men,
whereby we must
be saved</u>.

Acts 4:12

Satan

SATAN THE OLD DEVIL
What does God say about him?

The devil is the one that brings death, sadness, and makes terrible things happen. He comes to steal the dreams in your heart from God, then to completely kill anything that tries to make them happen. Finally, he makes sure to destroy them so that God's purpose for your life will never happen and people will not get saved. Remember that God can only give good things because he is bound by his word of goodness and love. Jesus came only to give life and a very good life, not just a life that barely helps you scrape by. He wants you super blessed so you can bless others.

The thief cometh not, but for to steal, and to kill, and to destroy: I am come that they might have life, and that they might have it more abundantly.   John 10:10

The bible says that anyone who sins on purpose and does evil things is of the devil because the devil has been sinning from the very beginning of time. This is why Jesus came so he could completely destroy all the evil works of the devil. Jesus' name is truly the most powerful name that has ever been named.

He that committeth sin is of the devil; for the devil sinneth from the beginning. For this purpose the Son of God was manifested, that he might destroy the works of the devil.   1 John 3:8

One day soon, the devil and his demons will be cast into the lake of fire and brimstone (Brimstone: a toxic flammable mineral that can be found on the shores of the Dead Sea) where the beast and false prophet will also be tormented along with him forever, day and night. And devil that deceived them was cast into the lake of fire and brimstone, where the beast and the false prophet are, and shall be tormented day and night for ever and ever.   Revelation 20:10

Make sure to always read your bible, pray, and be on guard to stand against evil because the one that hates you, the devil, is roaring around and stalking you like a lion does to his prey, just waiting to eat and completely destroy you for any little mistake you make. Be sober, be vigilant; because your adversary the devil, as a roaring lion, walketh about, seeking whom he may devour.   1 Peter 5:8

Obey God's word and follow his instructions. Make sure to not do evil things, always coming against anything the devil wants you to do. If you do this, he will go away from you, but if you don't, you will give him an open door to come in and destroy your life. Submit yourselves therefore to God. Resist the devil, and he will flee from you.   James 4:7

When you do evil things; such as lying and stealing, then God says that you're of your father the devil because he did all these bad things from the beginning and is a murderer. Whenever he speaks, you can be sure that it's a lie because he is the father of lies.

190

Ye are of your father the devil, and the lusts of your father ye will do. He was a murderer from the beginning, and abode not in the truth, because there is no truth in him. When he speaketh a lie, he speaketh of his own: for he is a liar, and the father of it.

John 8:44

_____
_____
_____
_____
_____
_____
_____
_____
_____
_____
_____

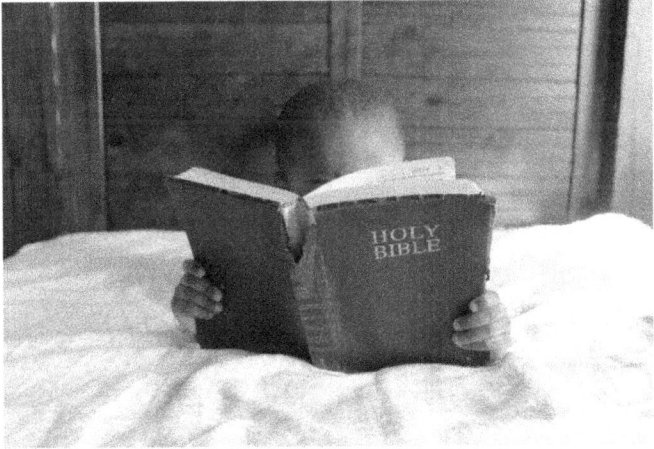

Where did it all start with the devil?

Who is this falling down & being kicked out of heaven by God, this son of the morning dawn who was named Lucifer! Being cut down like a tree, smack into the dark muddy ground, you who are very well known to make all nations weak and sad. You were so snooty and prideful wanting to be better and mightier than God that you said to yourself that you would ascend into heaven and make your glorious throne way above the stars of God. You said that you would make everyone praise you in areas of heaven being in charge of all the angels that meet on God's holy mountain. That you would climb higher than the highest clouds and be like God the most high. But what really happened to the devil was that God threw him down to the sides of hell and the deepest parts of the dark pit. At the end times, people will laugh staring and scratching their heads at him, wondering to themselves why the heck they were so afraid of the devil this whole time, saying, "Is this really the one that we were so afraid of, making the whole earth so terrified; trembling and shaking the entire world in fear?" "Is this the one that made the world into a horrible waste land, destroying all the cities that would not do his evil deeds?" Even kings of nations get decent burials when they die with words of honor at their funerals, but the devil's death will be like being thrown into a camp fire with no one caring to be there. Cast out like trash just like he'd done to all the people of the earth. The devil has left a legacy of death and sadness; therefore, he will never be honored.

How art thou fallen from heaven, O Lucifer, son of the morning! how art thou cut down to the ground, which didst weaken the nations! V. 13 For thou has said in thine heart, I will ascend into heaven, I will exalt my throne above the stars of God: I will sit also upon the mount of the congregation, in the sides of the north: V. 14 I will ascend above the heights of the clouds; I will be like the most High. V. 15 Yet thou shalt be brought down to hell, to the sides of the pit. V. 16 They that see thee shall narrowly look upon thee, and consider thee, saying, Is this the man that made the earth to tremble, that did shake kingdoms; V. 17 That made the world as a wilderness, and destroyed the cities thereof; that opened not the house of his prisoners? V. 18 All the kings of the nations, even all of them, lie in glory, every one in his own house. V. 19 But thou art cast out of thy grave like an abominable branch, and as the raiment of those that are slain, thrust through with a sword, that go down to the stones of the pit; as a carcase trodden under feet.   Isaiah 14:12-19

DID YOU KNOW...?

DID YOU KNOW that when the devil was in heaven he was a powerful cherub (angel) and very good at playing instruments? In fact, on the day he was created, God prepared for him timbrels and pipes which are musical instruments. Now the devil helps to make music really bad here on earth. Be careful what you listen to!
Ezekiel 28:13-15

DID YOU KNOW that Lucifer was the name that God gave the devil when God created him in heaven? Now most people just call him either the devil or Satan. Either way, he's defeated!
Isaiah 14:12

DID YOU KNOW that the devil cannot force you to do anything you don't allow him to do? In fact, he has to stay away from you if you resist him. This means that if you absolutely refuse to do the bad things he wants you to do, he *has* to go away.
James 4:7

DID YOU KNOW that Jesus, his disciples, and other Christians of that time cast out evil spirits from people? Jesus has called us to do the same. If someone is angry all the time or really depressed, it could be that a demon is causing them to feel this way through a stronghold. If someone is sick with a disease or is an alcoholic, it could be that a demon is causing the sickness. Look at this scripture regarding this subject.
Mark 16:17-18

Jesus told the evil spirit to come out of the child and it did. As soon as the evil spirit left, the child was healed right away. And Jesus rebuked the devil; and he departed out of him: and the child was cured from that very hour.

Matthew 17:18

A lot of people are afraid of the devil, so they do what he tells them to do out of fear. Others like to worship him and act like him. They even play around with evil games and things that scare them. The bible tells us that the devil has already lost every battle against us and God's kingdom. He lost because Jesus chose to die on the cross for us by shedding his precious blood.

Jesus

Self-Esteem

SELF-ESTEEM
Feeling Gross about Myself

Always do your best to dress up, wash yourself, and brush your hair. Look your best every day. Not only will this help you feel better about yourself, but others will appreciate you being clean. Also, by looking and smelling your best, you show that Jesus is taking care of you and meeting all of your needs. If you smell, people won't want to come near you, even though they may really like you a lot. When you have time, read what the Message version of the bible says about this scripture. It's great!

Let thy garments be always white; and let thy head lack no ointment. Ecclesiastes 9:8

No matter what I do in life; whether it is something very hard that I need to do or if I'm going through a difficult time with something or someone, I know that my help and strength comes from Jesus Christ. He gives me the strength to overcome every problem.

I can do all things through Christ which strengtheneth me. Philippians 4:13

We should never let our heart become sad or weary within us because though our bodies are becoming older, our true selves (our spirit) is becoming newer every single day as we read the word of God.

For which cause we faint not; but though our outward man perish, yet the inward man is renewed day by day. 2 Corinthians 4:16

Don't be sad or feel bad about yourself. Instead, be happy and have courage knowing that the Lord will strengthen your heart and soul, giving you his blessed hope that comes with an expected end of joy.

Be of good courage, and he shall strengthen your heart, all ye that hope in the Lord.   Psalms 31:24

I will always praise you because you took so much thought and creativity into making me so wonderfully. Your thoughts for me are so amazing and this I know for sure. Even when I was being formed in my mom's tummy, you could see me & were putting me together just the way you wanted me to be. You were making my bones, eyes, and toes grow; making sure to put them all where they belong. You made me exactly how you wanted me to look; knowing that the way I look would help me to fulfill exactly what you called me to do here on this earth for your purpose.

I will praise thee; for I am fearfully and wonderfully made: marvellous are thy works; and that my soul knoweth right well. V. 15 My substance was not hid from thee, when I was made in secret, and curiously wrought in the lowest parts of the earth. V. 16 Thine eyes did see my substance, yet being unperfect; and in thy book all my members were written, which in continuance were fashioned, when as yet there was none of them.
                                        Psalms 139:14-16

God has never and will never give us a spirit of fear, shyness, nervousness, panic, or worry. He gave us power and authority over fear and everything that comes with it, by his Holy Spirit. He has also put within us love and a

mind that is not only peaceful, but a mind that can understand things; while remembering lots of things.
For God hath not given us the spirit of fear; but of power, and of love, and of a sound mind.

2 Timothy 1:7

God cared about you so much that while you were still deep in your sins and hadn't asked Jesus to be the Lord of your life yet, he still died for you anyway. So if you sin and feel bad about yourself, ask God to forgive you as 1 John 1:9 says. When you repent and do your best to not do that sin again, you will feel so much better.
But God commendeth his love toward us, in that, while we were yet sinners, Christ died for us.   Romans 5:8

_____
_____
_____
_____
_____
_____
_____
_____
_____
_____
_____
_____
_____
_____
_____
_____

Sometimes we compare ourselves to others with
how they look, what they wear, or what
things they have that we don't. God
doesn't want us to do that because
he made us special just the way we
are. We are to be happy with
what we have. Our beautiful
faces look the way they
do because he knew it
would help to fulfill
his plan for
us on this
earth.

TESTIMONY: During a minister's conference when I was assisting in the sale of their books, I met a girl that had always wished to have blue eyes. One day, when she was invited to a village in another country to preach the gospel, only people with darker colored eyes could actually go into the village because the village people were too afraid of people with blue eyes. Since she was one of the few girls with brown eyes, she was able to go into the village and minister to the people there. Many of the villagers and their kids got saved! She never complained about her beautiful brown eyes again.

Prayer

Father God, I come to you in the name of Jesus. Your word says that I am worthy of your love. Help me to understand that I am made special just the way I am for your purposes here on this earth. Help me to look at myself as the amazing person that you made me.

I need your strength when I begin to feel not so pretty, overweight, or worthless. There are a lot of other people out there that seem to be smarter, look prettier, or seem to have everything. But inside, they're probably very sad, lonely, or insecure about things. Please help me to be happy and appreciate exactly how you made me. Besides, they may not be so perfect on the inside anyway. I repent for not appreciating who I am or how you made me. Thank you for your forgiveness and strength. Help me to love and see myself the way you love and see me...precious!

In Jesus Name...Amen

Sick

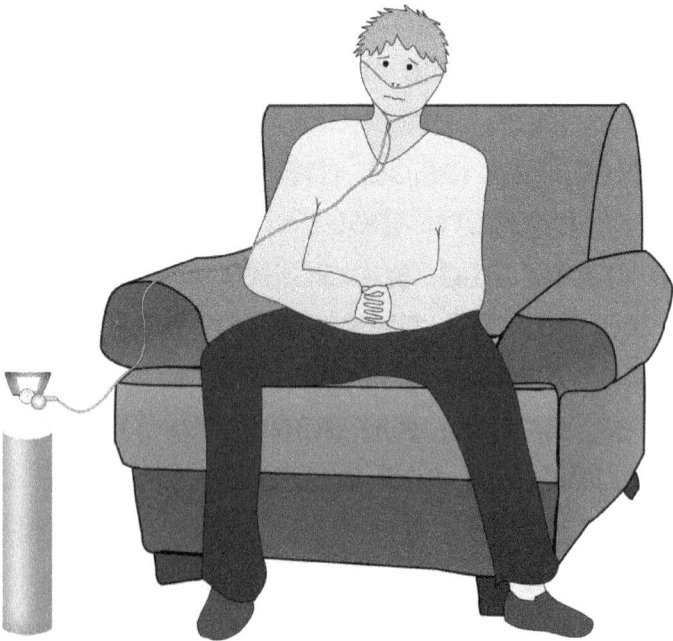

SICK
When I Am Not Feeling Good

Thank you, Lord! I prayed to you when I was deep in a horrible sickness and you heard my prayer and totally healed me. I was so weak but you made me strong again.
O Lord my God, I cried unto thee, and thou hast healed me. Psalms 30:2

Jesus was sent for us, healing everything in our bodies and hearts with his words. He rescued us from a life full of destruction.
He sent his word, and healed them, and delivered them from their destructions. Psalms 107:20

You endured all of our hurts and carried all of our deep sorrows. Yet, we didn't really care much about you. We were too busy deep in our sins. Nevertheless, you still chose to die for us, taking away all our hurts, poverty, sicknesses, diseases, and pain. The punishment we should have received you chose to put on yourself by your blood.
Surely he hath borne our griefs, and carried our sorrows: yet we did esteem him stricken, smitten of God, and afflicted. v. 5 But he was wounded for our transgressions, he was bruised for our iniquities: the chastisement of our peace was upon him; and with his stripes we are healed. Isaiah 53:4-5

If I'm sick, I can go to the leaders in my church and have them pray for me with oil in the name of Jesus. I know that if I believe, I'll be healed and get better. God will forgive me of my sins, too.

Is any sick among you? let him call for the elders of the church; and let them pray over him, anointing him with oil in the name of the Lord: v. 15 And the prayer of faith shall save the sick, and the Lord shall raise him up; and if he have committed sins, they shall be forgiven him.   James 5:14-15

If someone hurts my feelings, I know that Jesus will heal my broken heart, completely. I know he'll mend all of our hurts. Sometimes we don't only hurt on the outside, but we hurt on the inside. Jesus will heal it all.

He healeth the broken in heart, and bindeth up their wounds.   Psalms 147:3

Jesus doesn't only forgive us of all the sins we've ever done if we ask him to, but he also heals any and all sickness in our body. Hallelujah!

Who forgiveth all thine iniquities; who healeth all thy diseases.   Psalms 103:3

True peace can only come from Jesus. He heals our hearts with this peace. He does this for those near and even those far from him. He is always willing and able to heal you and even those that you love.

I create the fruit of the lips; Peace, peace to him that is far off, and to him that is near, saith the Lord; and I will heal him.   Isaiah 57:19

All that were blind and couldn't walk came to him in church. He healed every single one of them.

And the blind and the lame came to him in the temple; and he healed them. Matthew 21:14

Sickness only comes from the devil. When Jesus saw these people with sicknesses, he knew there were demons around so he cast them out and the people were not only healed but set free.

When the even was come, they brought unto him many that were possessed with devils: and he cast out the spirits with his word, and healed all that were sick. Matthew 8:16

God promises to give us a long and good life if we obey all the things he tells us to do. If we stay close to him, we will always be safe and protected by him and his angels. His promise to us is that we don't have to die young but stay healthy and strong for a very long time.

With long life will I satisfy him, and shew him my salvation. Psalms 91:16

When God raised Jesus from the dead, he sent the Holy Spirit to come down to earth so that we could be filled. He lives in us just as he lives in Jesus. The Spirit brings our bodies to life as he did to Jesus' body.

But if the Spirit of him that raised up Jesus from the dead dwell in you, he that raised up Christ from the dead shall also quicken your mortal bodies by his Spirit that dwelleth in you. Romans 8:11

When Jesus hung on the cross, he literally took all the sins of the world upon him so we could live in him. By his precious blood we are healed.

Who his own self bare our sins in his own body on the tree, that we, being dead to sins, should live unto righteousness: by whose stripes ye were healed.

1 Peter 2:24

It's important to always serve the Lord by obeying him and praying or singing songs. Many blessings will come if you do. God will bless your nourishment and take sickness far away from you & your family.

And ye shall serve the Lord your God, and he shall bless thy bread, and thy water; and I will take sickness away from the midst of thee.

Exodus 23:25

When you get saved and ask Jesus into your heart, God says that you will be able to be used by him. You can put your hands on someone and pray, commanding evil spirits to come out of them and they have to come out. You can also put your hands on sick people and command their bodies to be healed and they will be healed! The bible even says that if you accidentally drink something poisonous or accidentally get bit by a snake, you will not be hurt. God is so good.

He that believeth and is baptized shall be saved; but he that believeth not shall be damned. v. 17 And these signs shall follow them that believe; In my name shall they cast out devils; they shall speak with new tongues; v. 18 They shall take up serpents; and if they drink any deadly thing, it shall not hurt them; they shall lay hands on the sick, and they shall recover.

Mark 16:16-18

If you've been really sick in your mind or body, the Lord promises that he will make you completely better if you'll just trust him. If you got burned or cut yourself, he would heal all your wounds.

For I will restore health unto thee, and I will heal thee of thy wounds, saith the Lord; because they called thee an Outcast, saying, This is Zion, whom no man seeketh after.   Jeremiah 30:17

A lot of people would love to find the "fountain of youth" that makes them all better and young again, but there's no such thing in the world. Only God can make your body and mind stay young and healthy. When some people get older, they start to forget a lot of important things like who their families are. They even forget their whole life and worst of all, they forget how to love. However, if you read your bible everyday and keep his scriptures close to heart, they will be the secret to a wonderful life that brings healing to your mind and body as you read and hear them every day.

My son, attend to my words; incline thine ear unto my sayings. V. 21 Let them not depart from thine eyes; keep them in the midst of thine heart. V. 22 For they are life unto those that find them, and health to all their flesh.   Proverbs 4:20-22

One day a man came to Jesus that had a horrible disease on his skin. He was very contagious and could have given other people the same disease. He was supposed to stay in the camp with all the other people had the same disease but when he saw Jesus, he asked him if he was willing to heal him. Jesus said that he was indeed willing to heal him, so he did. The man immediately felt his skin heal and was so happy because he had no more pain and was going to live. Hallelujah!

<u>And, Behold, there came a leper and worshipped him, saying, Lord, if thou wilt, thou canst make me clean. V. 3 And Jesus put forth his hand, and touched him, saying, I will; be thou clean. And immediately his leprosy was cleansed.</u>   Matthew 8:2-3

_____
_____
_____
_____
_____
_____
_____
_____
_____
_____
_____
_____
_____
_____
_____
_____
_____
_____
_____
_____

Prayer

Father God, I come to you in the name of Jesus and thank you for all you've done for me. I am so thankful that you sent Jesus to die for me on the cross. Thank you, Jesus, for taking all my sins, sicknesses, and diseases away so that I would never have to have them. Because you took all of my sins at the cross, I can now have fellowship with you and go to heaven. I belong to you now and forever.

Thank you that in your name I have authority. So in the name of Jesus, I rebuke and command all sickness and disease to leave my body right now! I command every evil spirit that is trying to make me sick to go now! You have no right to be around me and you are trespassing! I declare that no evil weapon formed against me is going to happen and that I am healed by Jesus' stripes (blood that was shed).

In Jesus Name...Amen

Jesus said that all we have to do is lay our
hands on people when they're sick and
pray over them (in faith) so they can be
healed. We can also go to the
leaders of the church and
have them pray for us
as well. The prayer
said in faith
will make the
sick person
well.

Spiritual Battles

SPIRITUAL BATTLES
When I Am Being Attacked

Wear the full armor of God. Wear God's armor so that you can fight against the devil's clever tricks. Our fight is not completely against people on earth. We are actually at war with evil spirits; such as, rulers, authorities, and other powers of this world's darkness. We are fighting against the spiritual powers of evil in the heavenly places. That is why you need to put on God's full armor every day. God is not talking about a physical armor, but a spiritual one – strong in faith and his word. If you stay prepared this way, then on the day when the devil throws evil at you, you will be able to stand strong. So stand with the belt of truth tied around your waist, and on your chest wear the protection of right living. On your feet wear the good news of peace to help you stand strong. And also use the shield of faith with which you can stop all the burning arrows that come from the evil one. Accept God's salvation as your helmet. And holding up the sword of the Spirit which is the word of God.

Put on the whole armour of God, that ye may be able to stand against the wiles of the devil. v. 12 For we wrestle not against flesh and blood, but against principalities, against powers, against the rulers of the darkness of this world, against spiritual wickedness in high places. v. 13 Wherefore take unto you the whole armour of God, that ye may be able to withstand in the evil day, and having done all, to stand. v. 14 Stand therefore, having your loins gird about with truth, and having on the breastplate of righteousness; v. 15 and your feet shod with the preparation of the gospel of peace; v. 16 Above all, taking the shield of faith, wherewith ye shall be able to quench all the fiery darts of the wicked. v. 17 And take the helmet of salvation, and the sword of the Spirit, which is the word of God: v. 18 Praying always with all prayer and supplication in the Spirit, and watching thereunto with all perseverance and supplication for all the saints.   Ephesians 6:11-17

_____
_____
_____
_____
_____
_____
_____
_____
_____
_____
_____
_____
_____
_____
_____
_____
_____
_____
_____
_____
_____
_____

FULL ARMOR OF GOD

216

Standing for a Loved One to be Saved

When standing for a loved one to be saved...

It's easy to get discouraged when you're praying for someone you care about to be saved. You have to understand that God hears your prayers when you're praying according to his will. Please know that people asking Jesus into their heart is always God's will and God's heart; therefore, the most power force is:

Prayer...It is a powerful force in the lives of those you are praying for – so don't stop! You may see them running wild and doing very bad things in life, but understand that it is especially during these times that they need your prayers; regardless of whether they seem to want them or not. It's also important to know that the devil is the main problem when it comes to your loved ones coming to Jesus. Here are the words of Jesus:

Or else how can one enter into a strong man's house, and spoil his goods, except he first bind the strong man? and then he will spoil his house.

Matthew 12:29

Here, Jesus is trying to tell us that we must take authority in his name and make sure to bind the devil & his demons from our loved ones. Look at what else Jesus says about this subject:

Then saith he unto his disciples, The harvest truly is plenteous, but the labourers are few; Pray ye therefore the Lord of the harvest, that he will send forth labourers into his harvest."

Matthew 9:37-38

In other words, the word of God needs to get deep into a person's heart. God knows exactly which people to send across their path so they will listen; even if it has to be a person from another state or even country. When you speak God's word over this person, his word will not come back empty. Here's a scripture on that:

So shall my word be that goeth forth out of my mouth: it shall not return unto me void, but it shall accomplish that which I please, and it shall prosper in the thing whereto I sent it.

Isaiah 55:11

The bible says that the devil has blinded people's minds so that they won't believe in Jesus or the good news of the gospel:

In whom the god of this world hath blinded the
minds of them which believe not, lest
the light of the glorious gospel
of Christ, who is the image
of God, should
shine unto
them.

2 Corinthians 4:4

Pray that the Lord would open their spiritual eyes and give them a soft heart. One that can be moldable and easier to work with.

And I will give them one heart, and I will put a new spirit
within you; and I will take the stony heart out of
their flesh, and will give them an
heart of flesh.

Ezekiel 11:19

_____
_____
_____
_____
_____
_____
_____
_____
_____
_____

Prayer

Father God, I come to you in the name of Jesus and I pray for _____. You evil spirit working in my loved one's life and blinding them of the gospel and God's love, I bind you in the name of Jesus! I use my authority as a child of God and the name of Jesus against you and command you to stop your evil plans against _____.

According to the word of God, I ruin your plans and I enter in to deliver this person from your hands; so in the name of Jesus, you let go of their minds now!

Lord, I ask that you would send specific people across _____'s path so that they would listen. Please send those that are full of your word and can preach the gospel to them in love. Open the eyes of their heart so they can see and hear your gospel clearly.

I ask you all these things in faith and I thank you that you are faithful to answer my prayer.

In Jesus Name...Amen

Strength

STRENGTH
When I Feel Weak

Through Jesus, we can do all things because he gives us all the strength we need to go through this life victorious; whether in good times or hard times. We can be sure that his joy will be our strength.

<u>I can do all things through Christ which strengtheneth me.</u>   Philippians 4:13

People that choose to trust in the Lord will become strong all over again. They will be strong in their faith, bodies, and mind. They will be so strong that they'll be able to have the strength that the eagles have when they rise up high into the sky. They will be able to run and not get weak. They will be able to walk a victorious life as a Christian & rise above as an overcomer.

<u>But they that wait upon the Lord shall renew their strength; they shall mount up with wings as eagles; they shall run, and not be weary; and they shall walk, and not faint.</u>   Isaiah 40:31

It is our Lord God that works in you not only because he wants to help you, but because he wants to do what pleases him through you. He gives you the strength and power to overcome and succeed.

<u>For it is God which worketh in you both to will and to do of his good pleasure.</u>   Philippians 2:13

God promises that if you put your hope in him, that he will strengthen and put courage in your heart. Trust in him always and keep your hope with expectation. The hope the world gives us is a maybe, but the hope that comes from God has an expected end with promise.

Be of good courage, and he shall strengthen your heart, all ye that hope in the Lord. Psalms 31:24

The Lord is the source of my brightness whenever I walk through dark times in my life. He is also my deliverer and rescuer. Who am I afraid of anyway? In him I have strength and I don't need to fear because he is the power & protection of every single part of my life.

The Lord is my light and my salvation; whom shall I fear? the Lord is the strength of my life; of whom shall I be afraid? Psalms 27:1

The Lord God is my every bit of strength when I feel weak in my mind and body. He is the cheerful song in my heart and has become my very rescue during these times. He is my salvation in whom I find my deliverance, prosperity, and healing.

The Lord is my strength and song, and is become my salvation. Psalms 118:14

Blessings to our God, the Father of our Lord Jesus Christ, the wonderful Father of forgiveness and mercy and the God of all comfort. He comforts us during the hardest times of our lives and knows that with this same comfort and peace he gives us, we will be able to show others this same comfort ourselves.

Blessed be God, even the Father of our Lord Jesus Christ, the Father of mercies, and the God of all

comfort; v. 4 Who comforteth us in all our tribulation, that we may be able to comfort them which are in any trouble, by the comfort wherewith we ourselves are comforted of God.   2 Corinthians 1:3-4

I am so thankful to Christ Jesus our Lord, who has given me the gifts and talents for the work he's called me to do. He knew I would be faithful to do them. He also knew that I could be trusted and has counted me faithful to look after the ministry of taking care of his people.

And I thank Christ Jesus our Lord, who hath enabled me, for that he counted me faithful, putting me into the ministry.   1 Timothy 1:12

The prosperity, healing, and deliverance of the righteous come from the Lord. This is for those who walk in God's obedient ways. He'll be their strength during times of trouble.

But the salvation of the righteous is of the Lord: he is their strength in the time of trouble.   Psalms 37:39

_____
_____
_____
_____
_____
_____
_____
_____
_____
_____

Prayer

Father God, I come to you in the name of Jesus and I thank you with all my heart for being my strength. I know that your joy gives me the strength I need to run this race as a Christian and to fulfill everything you've called me to do on this earth while I'm here. When I think about it, if your joy gives me strength, then you must really be a very happy person. Help me to be happy like you are since there are times that I feel like I have no strength to fight against the darkness in my life. Sometimes I get shy about telling others about you because I know I'll be made fun of. Please help me to be bold and strong during these times. Help me when I feel weak.

There's one more thing, sometimes when I am sick, I feel really weak then too. I can hardly stand and feel like a noodle. Please strengthen my body to become strong the way you designed it to be. I thank you that I am healed by Jesus' stripes both in my mind and body.

In Jesus Name...Amen

Draw a picture of a time you felt very weak...

Draw a picture of a time when you felt strong...

Tempted

TEMPTED
When I Feel Like Sinning

It doesn't matter what kind of temptation is out there, there isn't any new temptation that people don't know about. It's all the same temptations that everyone has ever known about. Remember that God is faithful to us and he helps us resist against the enemy. When you feel like sinning, God shows us the way out through his word. Trust him to give you the strength to overcome any sin calling out your name.

There hath no temptation taken you but such as is common to man: but God is faithful, who will not suffer you to be tempted above that ye are able; but will with the temptation also make a way to escape, that ye may be able to bear it.   1 Corinthians 10:13

Stay under the authority of God. Refuse to give in to the devil's lies and temptations. He will have no choice but to run away from you. When he comes back to bother you later, ignore him again.

Submit yourselves therefore to God. Resist the devil, and he will flee from you.   James 4:7

When someone feels like sinning and is being tempted, he cannot ever say he is being tempted by God because God cannot be tempted by evil, nor does he tempt any one, ever. People allow themselves to be tempted because they choose to. When they give in to the lust of temptation, it makes the sin happen – leading to spiritual death. And sometimes, even physical death.

Let no man say when he is tempted, I am tempted of God: for God cannot be tempted with evil, neither tempteth he any man. V. 14 But every man is tempted, when he is drawn away of his own lust, and enticed. V. 15 Then when lust hath conceived, it bringeth forth sin: and sin, when it is finished, bringeth forth death.

James 1:13-15

_____

_____

_____

_____

_____

_____

_____

_____

_____

_____

_____

_____

_____

_____

_____

_____

_____

_____

Circle the words that help you overcome sin and put a line through the words that are sin:

Praying   Fighting

unjust   Lying

Bible   Loving

Patience   Longsuffering

Hope   Strength

Resisting   Joy

Unforgiveness   Peaceful

Cheating   unfair

Push Away   Anger

Forgiveness   Walking in Love

Disobedience   Ignoring

Stealing   Power

Lust   Greed

Gossiping   Happiness   Give Into

Curse Words   Sin

Obedience   Overcome

Sometimes we are tempted to steal or to cheat on tests, but that is not what God wants us to do. He wants us to be strong and overcome evil with good. Pray when you feel tempted and God will help you.

Prayer

Father God, I come to you in the name of Jesus and confess to you that I have allowed myself to be tempted and have even sinned against you and myself. I apologize so much for giving in to temptation and for not ignoring the devil when he tempted me. I know that cheating, stealing, gossiping, and doing evil things are not right. They are wrong. I ask for your forgiveness. I also ask that you would please give me the strength to stay strong whenever I feel like I want to give in to the temptation of sin. I thank you that when I am weak, you are strong in me. I also thank you that your word says that if I will resist and ignore the devil, then he has to run away from me.

Thank you that you have forgiven me and still love me.

In Jesus Name...Amen

Thankful

THANKFUL
Being Grateful

I will always give thanks and call upon your name, Lord. You do so many wonderful things for us, so we will tell the world about it.

Give thanks unto the Lord, call upon his name, make known his deeds among the people.   1 Chronicles 16:8

There are many ways we can show thanks to you. We can sing or even play one of our instruments. Every morning we will praise you because every morning you show us your kindness and faithfulness.

It is a good thing to give thanks unto the Lord, and to sing praises unto thy name, O most High: To shew forth thy lovingkindness in the morning, and thy faithfulness every night, v. 3 Upon an instrument of ten strings, and upon the psaltery; upon the harp with a solemn sound.
Psalms 92:1-2

Even in the middle of the night, I will give thanks to you because your commands bring life to us and they are for our own good.

At midnight I will rise to give thanks unto thee because of thy righteous judgments.   Psalms 119:62

I will always make sure that everything I do or say will bring glory to Jesus; making sure to give thanks to our Father God in his name.

And whatsoever ye do in word or deed, do all in the name of the Lord Jesus, giving thanks to God and the Father by him. Colossians 3:17

Sometimes we may want to complain about things, but it is God's will that we be grateful and thankful for everything we have.

In everything give thanks: for this is the will of God in Christ Jesus concerning you. 1 Thessalonians 5:18

King David was always so thankful to the Lord that his heart would just burst out in thanksgiving during the day and night. Most of the time, he sang and played songs to him. He knew God's compassion and forgiveness lasts forever and that made him so happy.

Oh give thanks unto the Lord, for he is good: for his mercy endureth for ever. Psalms 107:1

No matter what we go through in life, always give thanks to God for all things in the name of his son Jesus. Be willing to serve each other because you love God.

Giving thanks always for all things unto God and the Father in the name of our Lord Jesus Christ; Submitting yourselves one to another in the fear of God.
Ephesians 5:20-21

Don't let anyone fool you. Only good things come from the Lord; not bad things like diseases or sicknesses. He came to give us a good life. God never changes. **Every good gift and every perfect gift is from above, and cometh down from the Father of lights, with whom is no variableness, neither shadow of turning.** James 1:17

Instead of worrying about things and getting nervous or scared, pray and talk to God about all the issues that are troubling your heart.

Be careful for nothing; but in everything by prayer and supplication with thanksgiving let your requests be made known unto God.   Philippians 4:6

Some people might tell you that it is not good to eat certain animals, but that is not what God says. He says that all animals are good to eat since Jesus died and rose again. As long as you pray and give thanks, God will make it holy and safe to eat.

For every creature of God is good, and nothing to be refused, if it be received with thanksgiving: v. 5 For it is sanctified by the word of God and prayer.
                                        1 Timothy 4:4-5

_____
_____
_____
_____
_____
_____
_____
_____
_____
_____
_____
_____
_____
_____

Prayer

Father God, I come to you in the name of Jesus and thank you that you made everything good for us. I thank you that only good and perfect gifts come from you. Every day I will thank you with my voice and in other ways that I know to do; like playing an instrument for you. In Psalms, I read that King David wrote a lot of songs for you out of his heart of thanksgiving. I will also make music and sing unto you, too.

Father, please give me a heart of thankfulness for what I have. Help me not be anxious or nervous about anything. Please help me to trust you and know that you care about me and everything that I go through. In Jesus name, I declare that I will walk in peace and be full of thanksgiving for all the Lord has done for me. I command the spirit of stress and anxiety to leave me now.

In Jesus Name...Amen

Trust

TRUST
When I Need to Trust You More

There's only one person we should trust more than anyone else and that's the Lord. We should not trust in our own hearts, but lean into *his* heart who knows what's best for us. He will show us the right paths to take as long as we ask him to lead us.

Trust in the Lord with all thine heart; and lean not unto thine own understanding. v. 6 In all thy ways acknowledge him, and he shall direct thy paths.

Proverbs 3:5-6

I know we sometimes want things to happen right away, but the Lord tells us to be patient and brave while standing steadfast on his promises. He will help us to stay strong and to obtain the courage that we need. Remember that during this time we grow spiritually.

Wait on the Lord: be of good courage, and he shall strengthen thine heart: wait, I say, on the Lord.

Psalms 27:14

If someone gives you really bad news about anything, don't be afraid. Be strong in your trust towards the Lord so that when bad news comes, you will not be moved. You will stay strong in faith.

He shall not be afraid of evil tidings: his heart is fixed, trusting in the Lord.

Psalms 112:7

God has a plan for your life. Trust that he will make sure to help you every step of the way to finish that plan successfully.

Being confident of this very thing, that he which hath begun a good work in you will perform it until the day of Jesus Christ.   Philippians 1:6

Jesus Christ never changes. He's the same yesterday, today, and forever. **Jesus Christ the same yesterday, and to day, and for ever.**   Hebrews 13:8

_____
_____
_____
_____
_____
_____
_____
_____
_____
_____
_____
_____
_____
_____
_____
_____
_____
_____
_____
_____
_____
_____

Prayer

Father God, I come to you in the name of Jesus and thank you that you are on my side. I know that your word says that you know what's best for us and that we should be of good courage trusting you with every part of our lives, so please forgive me when I stop trusting you. I only mess things up when I don't obey your words. Thank you for keeping my heart strong and steady. You are my everything and I will trust you with all my heart.

In the name of Jesus, today I make the choice to stop putting my trust in things or people that speak the opposite of God's word. I know that you keep me safe in the palm of your hand; therefore, I command doubt to go! I will trust in the Lord always.

In Jesus Name...Amen

When was a time you chose not to trust in the Lord and leaned on your own ways to help you? How did that turn out?

_____

_____

_____

_____

_____

_____

_____

_____

_____

_____

_____

_____

_____

_____

_____

_____

_____

Wisdom

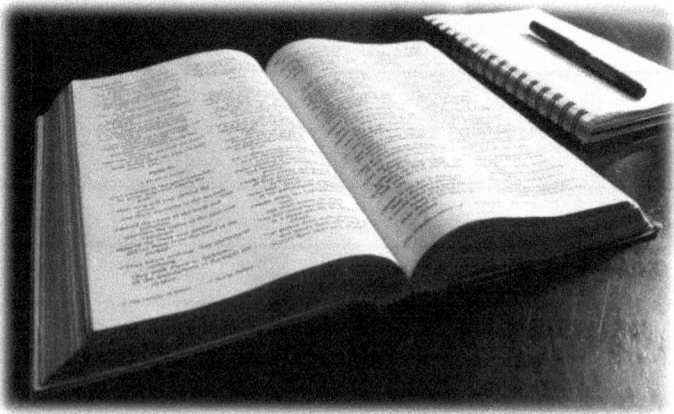

WISDOM
Understanding & Knowing Things

Don't ever let the written words from God's Holy Bible leave your heart and mouth. Study and say them day and night so that you will make sure to always have the wisdom to obey what it says. If you keep God's word a part of your everyday life, you will be prosperous. You will also be smart and successful.

<u>This book of the law shall not depart out of thy mouth; but thou shalt meditate therein day and night, that thou mayest observe to do according to all that is written therein: for then thou shalt make thy way prosperous, and then thou shalt have good success.</u>

Joshua 1:8

God's holy word will show you the right way you should go. It will also show you what you must do for your everyday life. Your whole life's purpose here on this earth is found with the Lord.

<u>That the Lord thy God may shew us the way wherein we may walk, and the thing that we may do.</u> Jeremiah 42:3

Pray so that you can speak in a way that will be completely clear to those hearing the gospel as it should be told so they will understand quickly, knowing the time is short.

Pray that your words will always be full of God's power and hope, giving every different person the answers they need to know about salvation.

That I may make it manifest, as I ought to speak. v. 5 Walk in wisdom toward them that are without, redeeming the time. v. 6 Let your speech be always with grace, seasoned with salt, that ye may know how ye ought to answer every man.   Colossians 4:4

If you need wisdom for something important, ask God who loves to give wisdom. He will give you the answers you're looking for. But, make sure that when you ask, you ask in faith believing that you will receive the wisdom you've asked for. Don't doubt or you will be like a boat being tossed around by the wind all over the ocean. You will not receive your answer from the Lord if you doubt because God says that a man that says he believes, then turns right around and doubts, is like an unstable person that has two ways of thinking. They always change their minds about things; failing at a lot of things in their life. Even their thinking about the word is questioned, so they begin to compromise on good or bad decisions.

If any of you lack wisdom, let him ask of God, that giveth to all men liberally, and upbraideth not; and it shall be given him. v. 6 But let him ask in faith, nothing wavering. For he that wavereth is like a wave of the sea driven with the wind and tossed. v. 7 For let not that man think that he shall receive any thing of the Lord. v. 8 A double minded man is unstable in all his ways.
                                                    James 1:5-7

Always remember that the wisdom you will ever get from God is first going to be pure, then full of peace, gentle, full of mercy, having a good outcome, not showing favoritism over another, and sincere. If wisdom is evil or comes any other way than these ways, then you know it is from the devil.

But the wisdom that is from above is first pure, then peaceable, gentle, and easy to be entreated, full of mercy and good fruit, without partiality, and without hypocrisy. James 3:17

God's people are damaged because they lack understanding of his word which is their path in life. God's people are lost because their knowledge of him is limited by their own choosing. In the Old Testament, God was sad that his people had rejected and forgotten everything about his words. They stopped following him altogether, so he couldn't bless their families the way he really wanted to.

My people are destroyed for lack of knowledge: because thou hast rejected knowledge, I will also reject thee, that thou shalt be no priest for me: seeing thou hast forgotten the law of thy God, I will also forget thy children. Hosea 4:6

_____

_____

_____

_____

_____

_____

_____

Worried

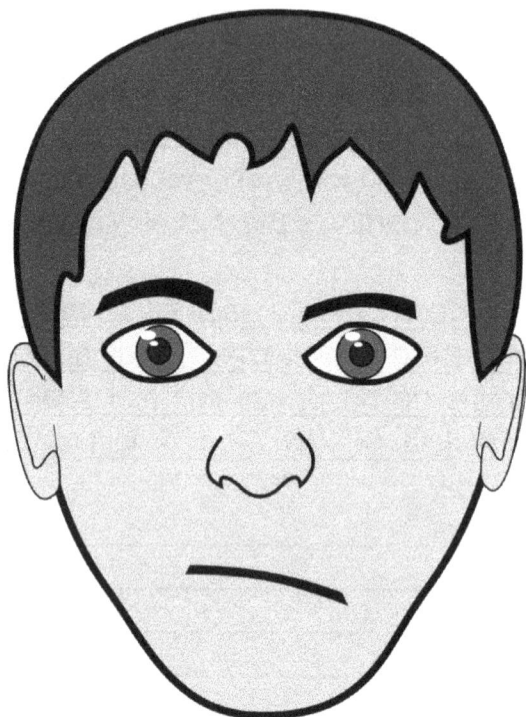

WORRIED
When I Feel Worried or Stressed

If you feel really worried and nervous about something, just give it to God. He cares so much and doesn't want you to feel stressed. He knows stress can cause all sorts of sicknesses to your body & mind. Plus, he really wants you to trust him because he cares for you.
Casting all your care upon him; for he careth for you.
1 Peter 5:7

Don't let yourself get scared about things. Not even the dark. God is always with you, even if you don't see him. You are never alone. If you're going to take a hard test or something, he'll be there to give you the peace and wisdom that you need. He will hold you close. **Fear thou not; for I am with thee: be not dismayed; for I am thy God: I will strengthen thee; yea, I will help thee; yea, I will uphold thee with the right hand of my righteousness.** Isaiah 41:10

When God tells us to be careful for nothing, he is telling us to not be anxious and worried about things. Instead, he wants us to pray about things so he can hear you and help you. The next time you're worried and feel like you are having a panic attack...trust and pray.
Be careful for nothing; but in everything by prayer and supplication with thanksgiving let your requests be made known unto God. Philippians 4:6

God does not give us things that will scare us. Nor will he ever make you do something to make you scared. Only the devil does that. God gave us his spirit that is full of power and of his kind love, so you can have peace in your mind; not being worried or scared.

For God hath not given us a spirit of fear; but of power, and of love, and of a sound mind.   2 Timothy 1:7

_____
_____
_____
_____
_____
_____
_____
_____
_____
_____
_____
_____
_____
_____
_____
_____
_____
_____
_____
_____
_____
_____
_____
_____

Did you know that when you're worried about something <u>you're</u> <u>not</u> <u>in</u> <u>faith</u>? It's considered disobedience to God because you do not trust him to take care of whatever situation you're having. So the next time you're tempted to worry or stress about an issue, remember that God loves you and is there to help you through anything you may be facing. Don't even confess words like "worry" or "stress" over yourself. Confess only faith-filled words. *After all, even boys get tempted to worry just as much as girls (wink). Be strong in the Lord in everything!

The last time I felt really worried was when I...

_____

_____

_____

_____

_____

_____

_____

_____

_____

I think a better way I could have handled it is by ...

_____

_____

_____

_____

_____

_____

_____

_____

_____

Prayer

Father God, I come to you in the name of Jesus and thank you that I can pray to you anytime I feel worried, anxious, or stressed out. I know that worrying is a sin because it means I'm not trusting you. Sometimes I just really get anxiety over things like taking a test or performing at a school concert. Every time I start a new grade, I get super nervous then as well. My stomach starts hurting and my heart starts pounding. It doesn't feel good.

Father God, please help me to learn to trust you during these times. Help me to know that I'm never alone and that you're always with me. Help me to learn that you are my refuge and my strength...no matter what. I want to show others that during really hard times in our lives, we can have that peace that passes all human understanding; therefore, I command the spirit of fear to leave me now. Peace, be still.

In Jesus Name...Amen

Zacchaeus

Zacchaeus

Have you ever been to a parade and couldn't see anything because everyone in front of you was taller? How did it make you feel?

_____

_____

Do you think you would have been as excited to see Jesus as Zacchaeus was?

_____

_____

Zacchaeus felt super excited when Jesus was nearby. He wanted to see him so bad that he decided to run ahead of Jesus and climb up a sycamore tree!

The bible tells us that Zacchaeus lived in Jericho. He was not a very tall man. In fact, he was very short. He was a very wealthy Chief Tax Collector. One day he was trying very hard to see who Jesus was, but couldn't see over everyone's heads.

And, behold, there was a man named Zacchaeus, which was the chief among the publicans, and he was rich. V. 3 And he sought to see Jesus who he was; and could not for the press, because he was little of stature. V. 4 And he ran before, and climbed up into a sycomore tree to see him: for he was to pass that way. V. 5 And when Jesus came to the place, he looked up, and saw him, and said unto him, Zacchaeus, make haste, and come down; for to day I must abide at thy house.   Luke 19:2-5

Can you guess what happened after Jesus went to Zaccaeus' house?

Zaccaeus climbed down from the tree as Jesus had asked him to do. Jesus then went to his house and Zaccaeus got saved that day. He repented of all his sins and then even went a step further than that. Because he was so grateful and happy to have been set free of all his many sins, he decided to give back all the money that he had stolen from the people while collecting their taxes. It was a lot of money, but he didn't care. He was happy to give it all back. **Can you imagine how happy those people were to be getting money they weren't expecting?** I'm sure God answered many money prayers that day. Just think...Zaccaeus decision to follow Jesus helped a lot of people that wonderful day!

Have you ever cheated or stolen anything from anyone or any store? If so, could you have given it back and apologized? What would the Lord have wanted us to do?

_____

_____

_____

_____

_____

_____

_____

_____

_____

_____

Highlight the picture below with a yellow highlighter so you can see how bright Zaccaeus' house got that day...!

Coloring Pages...

Study Notes

www.ingramcontent.com/pod-product-compliance
Lightning Source LLC
LaVergne TN
LVHW011910080426
835508LV00007BA/334